CHARACTER

Books by Robert L. Dilenschneider

Character★

The Ultimate Guide to Power & Influence

Nailing It★

Decisions★

The Critical First Years of Your Professional Life★

50 Plus!★

The Critical 2nd Phase of Your Professional Life★

Power and Influence

Civility in America

The Public Relations Handbook

A Briefing for Leaders

The AMA Handbook of Public Relations

A Time for Heroes

Values for a New Generation

On Power

The Men of St. Charles

The Corporate Communications Bible

The Hero's Way

★Available from Kensington Publishing Corp.

What People Are Saying About Robert L. Dilenschneider and His Books

DECISIONS
Practical Advice from 23 Men and Women Who Shaped the World

"Upgrade your daily decisions with the wisdom of two dozen renowned influencers who changed history."
—**Mehmet Oz, MD,** Emmy Award–winning host of *The Dr. Oz Show*

"Sound advice wrapped in often little-known stories of a broad range of people from JFK to Ignaz Semmelweis. Fun to read and sound."
—**Fay Vincent,** former commissioner of Major League Baseball

"This supremely thoughtful book will help any reader to think more clearly about the decisions they face and, crucially, about the contexts in which those decisions must be made."
—**Bill Emmott,** former editor in chief, *The Economist*

"*Decisions* is a truly inspiring book about how to become a leader. Highly recommended!"
—**Douglas Brinkley,** *New York Times* bestselling author of *American Moonshot: John F. Kennedy and the Great Space Race*

"The best decision you will make today is to read and learn from this array of bold thinkers. Bob Dilenschneider offers remarkable insights that give new perspectives on our own decisions, large or small."
—**Harvey B. Mackay,** author of the #1 *New York Times* bestseller *Swim with the Sharks Without Being Eaten Alive*

THE CRITICAL FIRST YEARS OF YOUR PROFESSIONAL LIFE

"Dilenschneider knows that the first fourteen years of your professional life, properly managed, will propel you forward for the rest of your career. Whether the economy is weak or strong, he will help you navigate through the changing tides."
—**Maria Bartiromo,** host of *Mornings with Maria*

"Practical advice on how young people can take charge of their careers and develop independently both the skills required to excel in any environment and the savvy to know when to move on."
—**Norman R. Augustine,** former chairman and CEO of Lockheed Martin Corporation

"An insightful, idea-laden, practical guide that will be valuable to young professionals seeking to advance their on-the-job lives."
—**Stephen A. Greyser,** Richard P. Chapman Professor of Business Administration, emeritus, Harvard Business School

"This book is for anyone who wishes to make his or her mark in the business world. Bob Dilenschneider . . . shares strategic advice and years of tested experience with younger people who are just bringing their unpolished talents to the marketplace."
—**Reverend Theodore M. Hesburgh,** president emeritus, University of Notre Dame

"This book should be essential reading for young people starting out on a business career."
—**Henry Kaufman,** Henry Kaufman & Company, Inc.

CHARACTER

LIFE LESSONS IN COURAGE, INTEGRITY, AND LEADERSHIP

ROBERT L. DILENSCHNEIDER

Foreword by
Mitzi Perdue

CITADEL PRESS
Kensington Publishing Corp.
kensingtonbooks.com

CITADEL PRESS BOOKS are published by

Kensington Publishing Corp.
900 Third Avenue
New York, NY 10022

All Kensington titles, imprints, and distributed lines are available at special quantity discounts for bulk purchases for sales promotions, premiums, fundraising, educational, or institutional use. Special book excerpts or customized printings can also be created to fit specific needs. For details, write or phone the office of the Kensington sales manager: Kensington Publishing Corp., 900 Third Avenue, New York, NY 10022, attn Sales Department; phone 1-800-221-2647.

10 9 8 7 6 5 4 3 2 1

First Citadel trade paperback printing: April 2025

Printed in the United States of America

ISBN: 978-0-8065-4312-3

ISBN: 978-0-8065-4313-0 (e-book)

To Bruce, Logan, and Hailey

We are counting on you

CONTENTS

FOREWORD

Mitzi Perdue, widow of the poultry magnate Frank Perdue, is a war correspondent who writes about Ukraine. After her most recent stint there, she founded a crowdfunding effort, DonorSee.com/Ukraine, to help clear land mines from the region. When asked why she's doing this at an age when many have chosen to retire, she answers, "I'm influenced by Mother Teresa's words: The good that we can do, we must do."

If you and I were to meet in person, and it was evening, and maybe there was an adult beverage or two involved, I might work the conversation around to a discussion of what each of our visions of an ideal world would be. I've asked this question to enough people to know that there's tremendous variety in the possible answers that may occur to you.

Some people have said that their ideal world would be one in which there was no more war. For others, it might be education for everyone. For others, it would be the flourishing of the arts or, maybe better, health care for everyone, or maybe their ideal world would include having the underserved better supported, or better stewardship of the environment.

For some, it was more personal. Some people have told me their ideal world is one in which they get to be the best parent they can be, or perhaps one in which they serve their community or a cause they care about.

What would your answer be?

It matters, because your answer will reveal a lot about what you value, and in the process, your answer will also reveal in-

formation about who you really are. What you care about is a
window into your character.

My own answer is "An ideal world would be one in which
everyone gets to be all they can be."

Since, by nature, I have at least a somewhat practical bent,
my follow-up question to myself and to you is, "Given your vision for an ideal world, how would you get there?"

A big part of my answer to that question is "Inspiration!"

It's inspiration that helps us to think bigger than we've ever
thought before, and it's inspiration that can give us the energy
and the road map for getting where we want to be.

And now we come to what this foreword is really about!

The thirty-one profiles you are about to read are about people who are exceptional exemplars of character. They're inspirational because they used their abilities at their highest levels to
work for causes they believed in. Because of character, they influenced the world for good.

When you read this book, you're almost bound to be influenced by one or more of the profiles. Reading about admirable
people is like creating little computer programs in your head
that guide you to stretch further and to do more to live up to
what you're capable of. By raising your sights higher, you have
a golden chance to express your character at its best, and in so
doing, lead a fuller, more satisfying life. (Not a bad outcome, in
my opinion!)

Reading about inspirational people enables you to do what
Charlie "Tremendous" Jones, the great advocate for reading, used
to say: "In five years, you'll be the same person you are today
except for the people you meet and the books you read." The
book provides the vision to transcend day-to-day living and
embrace the chance to use your talents and abilities at their
highest level to make the world a better place. It's a chance to
encourage the highest and best aspects of your character.

What exactly are we aiming at, as we learn from these inspirational examples?

In the course of examining character, Robert Dilenschneider invites us to look at some of the components of character. His list includes:

- Leadership
- Innovation
- Resilience
- Breaking barriers
- Courage
- Loyalty
- Integrity
- Openness and transparency

None of us is going to excel in all these characteristics. But as you read this book, allow inspirational ideas to seep into your consciousness and, for that matter, your unconscious as well. When you do this, you'll have a better chance at what we all want, which is at the end of our days to feel that we've led a good and fulfilling life.

One of the threads to look for in each of the thirty-one stories of character is that none of these individuals had it easy. None had fame or fortune or world-changing influence drop in their laps.

All of these individuals overcame adversity on the way to becoming all they could be.

This makes me think of a saying that I often heard my late husband, Frank Perdue, use: "Adversity breeds character: Prosperity breeds monsters." I had a college experience that makes me believe the saying is true. The professor from a long-ago psychology class at Harvard asked us, his students, to write a ten-page autobiography.

After we had dutifully written and handed in our assignments, we learned that the purpose of writing our biographies wasn't to show how well-organized we were or what good writers we were, or what insights we had into our own characters. Rather, we were part of the professor's research project, one he had already been pursuing for decades.

His premise was that getting into Harvard takes drive and a steely willingness to try even when the odds of success were daunting. He believed that the resilience it took even to tackle the job of getting into Harvard implied a lot of character.

With that in mind, he told us that after reading thousands of his students' autobiographies, he had seen that every one of the papers revealed that the writer had endured some kind of character-forming adversity. These included such incidents as having a beloved brother who hanged himself. Another had a sister with schizophrenia. Still another had survived incest. Others had endured a very public family bankruptcy, and one recalled being shuffled from relative to relative because his parents were incarcerated. In one way or another, each of his students had struggled with and overcome serious, life-changing adversity.

So again, as you read through the profiles in this book, pay attention to the fact that each of these people whose characters we admire transcended adversity. In your own life, perhaps you have experienced "what doesn't kill me makes me stronger."

There's another thread to look for in each of the people profiled in this book. Each one of the individuals was a giver more than a taker. They gave back to the world and made it a better place. To put this in context, here's a quick story about the fourth person showcased in this book: Mother Teresa.

To understand her better, look at a person whose life stood in contrast with hers: Emperor Napoleon. A little more than two hundred years ago, Emperor Napoleon had more of the world's goodies than anyone else has ever had. He ruled most of Europe. He had palaces and jewels and women and glamour and status and fame and glory to a degree that is almost unimaginable. This is a man who you'd think had it all.

How different Mother Teresa's life was. Because of her vow of poverty, her material possessions consisted of nothing more than three cotton saris and the sandals on her feet. She ate the meager rations of the poor. She ministered to the poorest of the poor, taking care of lepers as they died. Her life was characterized by service, self-sacrifice, and worship.

Which of these two had happier lives?

We don't have to guess. At the end of his days, while exiled on Saint Helena, the remote volcanic island in the South Atlantic, Napoleon confided to a companion that when he looked back on his life, he couldn't count five consecutive happy days.

Mother Teresa, on the other hand, saw her life as one of "unending joy."

All that Napoleon had, he got by taking. Everything Mother Teresa had—love, approval, fame—she received by giving. My late mother used to say, "The givers of the world are happy. The takers of the world are miserable." Mother Teresa was a giver, and so were or are each of the individuals you'll be reading about.

None of us can emulate all these men and women, but if you allow yourself to be influenced by even one of them, you will be further ahead in the game of life. If you are influenced by several of them, guaranteed, not only your own life will be more fulfilling but you'll contribute more to those around you and, eventually, to every life you touch.

Whatever your definition of an ideal world, allow the men and women you're about to read about inspire you to play even a small role in bringing about a better world.

I'd like to end with a quote I learned in childhood. It summarizes why character is so important and why the study of it matters:

He who loses money, loses nothing.
He who loses health, loses something.
He who loses character loses everything there is.

Enjoy the following studies in character! And may they inspire you!

Chapter One

WHAT IS CHARACTER?

I have a dream that my four little children will one day live
in a nation where they will not be judged by the color of
their skin but by the content of their character.
—Martin Luther King Jr., March on Washington,
August 28, 1963

Dr. King's most famous line from his most famous speech
implores us to judge people not by superficial appearance but
rather by a more substantive measure: their character. How
many times have you thought that a politician or a celebrity or
a star athlete didn't seem particularly admirable because of
how they looked or what they said or what they did? What
most likely bothered you, even if unconsciously, was a lack of
some character trait such as honesty, integrity, or courage that
we all can instinctively recognize. It's like the old saying: I
may not know about art, but I know what I like.

Polls consistently show that most Americans believe our
country is headed in the wrong direction and that national
unity is in jeopardy. People know that something is wrong
and they are looking for guidance on how to get America
back on track.

> Character is like a tree and reputation its shadow. The shadow is what we think of it; the tree is the real thing.
>
> —Abraham Lincoln

This book will offer such guidance by helping you identify leaders who display the essential traits of character and suggest role models to use in your own lives. The United States and indeed the world are in urgent need of leadership in virtually every area: politics, business, social direction, nonprofits, and more. That leadership will be marked by "character," and this book will offer vignettes of men and women who reflected this quotient.

But what exactly is character?

The dictionary defines it as the mental and moral qualities distinctive to an individual, the distinctive nature of something, the quality of being individual in an interesting or unusual way, strength and originality in a person's nature, and a person's good reputation.

But beyond these definitions, we know that character is manifested in leadership, innovation, resilience, change, courage, loyalty, breaking barriers, and more. Character drives the best traits in our society, such as honesty, integrity, leadership, and transparency, and it drives others to exhibit those qualities.

While many of these characteristics seem to be missing in today's society, including in its leaders, all of you can elevate society by recognizing and incorporating the lessons of these vignettes into your own lives, which will inspire the lives of those around you.

I almost always, sometimes unconsciously, observe and judge the character of clients, employees, and even friends. I don't give demerits or merit badges, but I do find it useful to know who I'm dealing with, the level of trust I can bestow, and in the case of friends and employees, drop some helpful hints to help them build character. In many cases, I can make the right decision myself, leading by example, to show them how to solve a problem or resolve a crisis the correct way.

It's often said that bad luck or adverse circumstances help one build character. We learn from our mistakes or when bad things happen. Indeed, many of the diverse group of people we're going to examine were afflicted by disease, found themselves in war, imprisoned for political beliefs, or suffered personal or business setbacks from which they bounced back. But character doesn't always arise from adversity; it is fundamentally the choices we make in our lives that determine our character.

This book will examine the lives of thirty-one individuals who exhibited outstanding character in fields as diverse as politics, religion, medicine, business, sports, entertainment, and the military. Their stories will highlight their attributes and achievements, which have shaped our age. They will also offer a blueprint for future leaders to display much-needed character at a time when it seems lacking in many of those fields.

This is a big problem, and it defies an easy solution.

We desperately need courage, integrity, and leadership to face increasingly complicated problems, such as climate change, pandemics, war, and inequality. But too often serious voices offering solutions are drowned out on social media or in the public square by disinformation spread by those motivated more by ideology, prejudice, or ignorance. Consider this book as a guide to promoting positive discussion and finding solutions that work for everyone.

By studying these stories, and then delving deeper into the lives of these exemplars, I hope you'll find both hope and a blueprint of what character is and can achieve, and how to recognize and cultivate character in future leaders, including yourselves.

In some ways, our more complicated problems demand even stronger character and moral leadership and innovation and integrity than what is displayed by the people profiled in this book. Where is it going to come from? Hopefully, from you and those whose lives you guide and touch.

You'll find in this book detailed portraits of high-character individuals, each showcasing a different aspect that they embodied in their personal and professional lives. Some, like Nelson Mandela and Mother Teresa, are known across the globe. Others, like Winston Churchill, have become historical touchstones. Still others, like Jimmy Stewart or Steve Jobs, are icons of their industries. Many others, like Edith Cavell or Frederick Banting, may be less familiar but no less worthy of examination.

> While it's not by itself a character trait, many of those I'll profile, plus numerous others, have been imprisoned for their political views. On our list we have Nelson Mandela, Emmeline Pankhurst, Anwar Sadat, and Václav Havel, as well as John McCain, a prisoner of war. Other famous prisoners include Mohandas K. Gandhi, Dr. Martin Luther King Jr., Oscar Wilde, and Alexei Navalny.

Where possible, I've quoted or paraphrased the subjects' own written or spoken words, from their speeches, their books, their TV or radio appearances, their newspaper interviews, or contemporary sources. I've also concentrated on their actions and achievements and then commented on those words and actions, relating them to my theme of character. Their words are theirs, mine are mine. Your interpretations may differ, but I appreciate your taking the time to consider mine.

We'll start with *Leadership*, an evident manifestation of character. It is the character of leaders that attracts followers, whether in a military company or on the national or international political stage. We'll focus on General Colin Powell (1937–2021), a pioneering Army officer and later secretary of state; Valéry Giscard d'Estaing (1926–2020), who as president of France helped transform both that nation and Europe; Anwar Sadat (1918–1981), who as president of Egypt lost his life after championing peace between Israel and its neighbors; Mother Teresa (1910–1997), the Albanian nun who steadfastly changed the world's ideas about the poor; and Dwight D. Eisenhower (1890–1969), a man of many roles, including university president, war leader and hero, and a quietly effective president of the United States. It was the focus and character of each of these individuals that led to real societal change. In each case, change wouldn't have happened without their skill, desire, and will.

Using the examples of three very different people, we'll then look at *Innovation*, with very different characters. Innovation takes special character traits, both in conceiving and developing new ideas and in getting those new ideas accepted in often hidebound companies and societies. Steve Jobs (1955–2011) brought a steely, near-maniacal, determination to the founding, near collapse, and refounding of Apple, all the while fighting the disease that would claim his life. His legacy is a company whose products literally changed how the world communicates. Canadian Frederick Banting (1891–1941) co-discovered insulin and sold the patent for $1 in the hope that it would be made freely available to diabetics, a display of character often sadly lacking today. Walt Disney (1901–1966) transformed the worlds of movies and amusement parks with a singular vision and tenacity that have often been imitated but rarely duplicated.

Resilience is an often-underestimated aspect of character that reflects the ability and stamina to overcome the direst adversity. Few people embody this aspect of character more than Nelson Mandela (1918–2013), who was imprisoned for twenty-seven years on South Africa's Robben Island and elsewhere and emerged to win election as the country's president on a platform of truth and reconciliation. So did Václav Havel (1936–2011), the president of Czechoslovakia and the Czech Republic, whose embrace of democracy over authoritarianism broke the ultimate barrier to freedom for his people. The American suffragette Susan B. Anthony (1820–1906) remained loyal to her cause despite terrible hardships and died before women got the vote here. Emmeline Pankhurst (1858–1928) was a British suffragette who also embodied resilience fighting for the vote for women in the U.K. and, as we'll see, in the United States. We'll then look at the remarkable life of Stephen Hawking (1942–2018), whose mind uncovered some of the most basic truths of cosmology after his body shut down from disease.

It is character that often enables individuals to *break barriers* that hold back progress, be it in sports, entertainment, science, or business. Margaret Chase Smith (1897–1995) was the first woman to serve in both houses of Congress and was a consistent voice of reason. Bill Russell (1934–2022) was the first Black NBA superstar and first Black coach, winning an incredible eleven NBA championships. Julia Child (1912–2004) was the first successful television chef, popularizing serious home cooking for a generation. Barriers broken by these pioneers have led thousands of others to follow in their footsteps, enriching us all.

Courage is a recognizable character trait, but one that occurs all too infrequently. In this chapter we'll look at the lives of British prime minister Winston Churchill (1874–1965) and tennis great Arthur Ashe (1943–1993), who displayed courage his entire life before succumbing to a case of AIDS transmitted by a blood transfusion. Baseball legend Lou Gehrig (1903–1941) embodied courage fighting ALS. Florence Nightingale (1820–1910) and Edith Cavell (1865–1915), British nurses during the Crimean War and World War I respectively, in their own ways transformed the nursing profession despite great peril to themselves and, in Cavell's case, being executed by German troops.

Loyalty is another character trait often notable by its absence. We'll look at Eleanor Roosevelt (1884–1962), who managed to wield enormous influence while supporting her husband's career; John Wooden (1910–2010), who produced many of college basketball's exemplars at UCLA; and John McCain (1936–2018), whose loyalty to his fellow soldiers in Vietnam shaped his entire life.

> You can easily judge the character of a man by how he treats those who can do nothing for him.
> — Johann Wolfgang von Goethe

Integrity seems to flow out of those who possess it. We'll look at Daniel Patrick Moynihan (1927–2003), an academic and politician who once famously remarked that people are "entitled to their own opinions, but not their own facts"; Margaret Thatcher, later Baroness Thatcher (1925–2013), the Iron Lady; and Paul Volcker (1927–2019), who guided the United States out of one of its worst recessions and in so doing won the respect of Wall Street and Main Street.

Persons of character generally are open and *transparent*. We'll look at examples of this trait, among them Katharine Graham (1917–2001), whose stewardship of the *Washington Post* through Watergate and other storms was a model for how a free press promotes transparency; Jimmy Stewart (1908–1997), an actor who often played persons of character, as in *Mr. Smith Goes to Washington*, and flew bombing missions for the U.S. Army and Air Force in World War II; and Theodore Hesburgh (1917–2015), whose integrity and openness as the president of the University of Notre Dame won him a national following.

We'll conclude with the remarkable life of S. P. Hinduja (1935–2023), who was born in the part of India that is now Pakistan and became one of the wealthiest men in the world through his various business enterprises. But it was not his financial success that defined him—it was his character. S. P. exemplified many of the traits we have discussed, such as leadership, loyalty, and integrity, that, combined with other qualities, created transcendence. We will describe what this means in the final chapter.

> All men make mistakes, but a good man yields when he knows his course is wrong and repairs the evil. The only crime is pride.
>
> —Sophocles, *Antigone*

Many of these people remain well known, some were once well known but have been passed over by history, and others were never really recognized for their accomplishments. It doesn't matter. Character is not something that exists only if recognized. But it is important—vital, really—that we learn from the lives and stories of others. Yes, as the philosopher George Santayana may have said, "Those who cannot remember the past are condemned to repeat it," but also, those who don't learn by example or have ideals and heroes are condemned to live less than fully successful lives.

Through these thirty-one portraits we'll show what character is (and what it isn't) and how having enough of at least one of these traits can determine success and make a person worthy of emulation. Many of these people display several of these traits. Striving toward imbuing these traits into your life and personality will help you become a better person and help our society heal.

Chapter Two

LEADERSHIP

Character, in the long run, is the decisive factor in the life of an individual and of nations alike.

—Theodore Roosevelt

Leadership is one of the most easily recognizable of character traits. A man or woman leads others by the quality of his or her character. The individual may be a military officer who has risen to the top based on the ability to get others to follow his ideas and orders. Or he may be a politician who compels support to gain power, but then uses that power for the good of the community and the world. Or she might be an individual whose moral force is so strong that others can't help but follow.

As Theodore Roosevelt is quoted above, individual character traits sometimes come to define whole nations, often unfairly. Think of snooty French waiters or punctilious Swiss or stiff-upper-lip British or overfriendly Americans. Or in your experience, you may have found French waiters to be charming and helpful, Swiss people to be sloppy, the British to be outgoing and friendly, and Americans to be morose. So while I'd never contradict Teddy Roosevelt, it pays to be cautious with generalizations.

In this chapter we'll stick with specific individuals and examine key parts of the lives of General Colin Powell, a military man turned statesman, whose character embodied the best of America;

Valéry Giscard d'Estaing, a politician who played a critical role in unifying a continent, defying the image of the insular French; Anwar Sadat, whose quest for Middle East peace took him well outside Egypt and cost him his life; Mother Teresa, a simple nun whose vision compelled her to leave the cloister and awaken the conscience of the world; and Dwight D. Eisenhower, who led his country and the world bravely in war and peace.

Each of these lives suggest lessons which I'll detail at the end of each section.

General Colin Powell

The day the soldiers stop bringing you their problems is the day you stopped leading them. They have either lost confidence that you can help them or concluded that you do not care. Either case is a failure of leadership.

That is a direct quote from Colin Powell.

Powell was invested in the idea of leadership. And as a four-star Army general, a national security advisor, a chairman of the Joint Chiefs of Staff, and a secretary of state, he personified leadership.

I met him one day when I was living in Tudor City, an enclave in Manhattan, and he was walking to the U.N. When we saw one another, we immediately walked together and then over the next several weeks took time in parks in Tudor City talking about some of the big ideas that were of interest to Powell, and to me.

It was early in my career, so I was talking about what I was going to do, and Powell made it clear that I should not have someone else make my choices. My choices should be my choices. But then he said, "Be careful what you chose." With a smile he added, "Someday you might regret it."

What was he alluding to? I could only guess at the time.

One day I was sitting outside 5 Tudor City Place and an argument was going on with two people in the street. Powell looked at me and said these guys are having a problem: They are going to be mad at one another but they need to get over it. That's a key to living a good life. Powell approached them. Talking to one in the middle of the argument, Powell said, "It is not as bad as you think, in fact it can look better in an hour from now."

He encouraged the men to remain calm and be kind. They looked surprised at this stranger giving them advice. But what a generous lesson it was. Talking about my future at another time, Powell encouraged me to have a vision, and to be demanding at every turn.

He also encouraged perpetual optimism and said that it is a "force multiplier." The term is from military science but applies in this case to a trait that can effectively spread exponentially in a group. Even if the situation is terrible, Powell believed, a leader must communicate optimism and reflect positive aspects.

To be sure, Powell avoided gloom and doom and instead spoke with optimism in his military speeches as well as when he was secretary of state. None of this was highly noted, however.

Powell always focused on being a realist and motivated me to do exactly the same. It is possible to be an optimist and a realist simultaneously. You are an optimist with others, inspiring them to be and do their best. But to yourself, you add a dose of realism so that you can anticipate obstacles and come up with a plan to address them.

It wasn't as though he were lecturing me; our conversations roamed across many subjects as he peppered them with encouragement and advice.

"I encourage you to be positive at every turn," he once told me, emphasizing again the value of optimism. "Don't let the naysayers deliver advice."

If you have fear—and who doesn't at times—deal with it on your own terms. It is yours, not anyone else's. Once you give someone else the power to control your fears, you lose your own control.

Lately I've been reflecting on those days in Tudor City when Powell described the basic principles related to leadership and how leadership mirrors character.

One day on Forty-Third Street, at the end of Tudor City, where there are long and steep steps leading down to First Avenue and the United Nations, I asked Powell if he was going to be okay going down those steps. He was older than me and I thought I was being courteous. He looked at me with a big smile and said, "I think I can do it." I trailed behind him huffing and puffing every step of the way.

He was a man of physical and intellectual vigor.

Colin Powell was born in Harlem to Jamaican immigrants, raised in the South Bronx, and studied at City College, where he joined the ROTC and was commissioned as a lieutenant in the Army. Powell recalled that in high school and college he worked as a clerk, as a seller of baby furniture at a store in the Bronx, where he learned enough Yiddish to later chat with the Israeli Prime Minister Yitzhak Shamir in his language.

I first heard about Colin Powell, then a young Black military officer, from Civil Rights leader Whitney Young, who was extremely close to someone I had a professional relationship with. Young told me "keep an eye" on this young man. I said, "But he is in the military." Young said, "Yes, but he won't stay in the military for long." And that turned out to be true.

Powell was the first Black chairman of the Joint Chiefs of Staff. He was also the youngest. He was also the first Black secretary of state. He was awarded the Presidential Medal of Freedom and the Congressional Gold Medal, along with dozens of other points of recognition. Powell strongly considered running for president in 2004 and 2008 but in the end decided not to do it because he just didn't want the job enough to withstand the campaign.

In those days of conversation in Tudor City, Powell talked about challenging himself, emphasizing the abilities needed to deal with tests of leadership. That sure worked for him in 1991, when he argued strongly for a decision to free Kuwait, despite the difficulties of fighting a war in a far-off desert without clear support from all sides. But that's U.S. politics, and this conflict established Powell's reputation as a leader.

Perhaps most important, Powell encouraged leaders to think for themselves and not automatically adopt someone else's good idea.

During the occasional meetings in Tudor City, Powell emphasized that to be a leader and to be optimistic you have to be practical in a way that leads to solutions and away from setbacks. He said that if a leader doesn't believe something is possible and demonstrates a way to achieve it, he likely won't succeed in the effort.

He said the leader knows how to evaluate situations and ask the right questions, such as: What can go wrong? If the solution is so good, why hasn't someone tried it before? What am I missing? These are basic proddings that could be applied to virtually everything he was involved in.

Powell encouraged me to separate my ego from my position. Keep your ego in check, he said; don't let it get the better of you. To be sure, Powell called for me and everyone else to have a healthy ego but to make decisions based on the facts and not colored by any personal interests.

He said it takes a strong character to admit mistakes and move on and leave ego out of it.

Speaking of mistakes, Powell led by example. In February 2003 he went before the United Nations and said the United States had intelligence showing that Saddam Hussein had "weapons of mass destruction" in Iraq. He used that phrase seventeen times in his speech.

His UN speech was notable because Powell, who was then secretary of state, had been a steadfast critic of any U.S. intervention with Iraq's leader.

But "weapons of mass destruction" became a catchphrase and a reason for the U.S. to invade Iraq, which led to decades of war and the deaths of nearly 4,500 Americans and more than 185,000 Iraqi civilians.

To be sure, Powell was said to be furious when he said intelligence experts had misled him about Saddam Hussein's capacity for the so-called weapons of mass destruction. None were ever found.

Powell resigned as secretary of state a year later. He said he regretted his role in the hasty decision to invade Iraq.

He used to say that leaders shouldn't harbor negative feelings. Easier said than done.

Perhaps the most important thing Powell taught me, something that I've applied to my career ever since, was that details matter. And don't be afraid to check and recheck even the smallest detail before proceeding. He said he learned this as a soldier but obviously he felt it would work in business and in politics and indeed throughout life. Powell also emphasized that it is important to praise and share accolades whenever possible, and to voice any criticism in private. "If you do this," he said, "people will follow."

It is also useful to take a few deep breaths, relax, and show compassion and understanding for others, rather than stress. If you can do this, you will be a leader whom everyone else respects.

As he stood up from our bench and began walking to the U.N. one morning, he said, "You need a clear and attainable objective, Bob. You have to be sure and have no second thoughts. You have to overcome adversity and move forward with certainty."

Based on all of this, the "Powell doctrine" was created—a term coined by journalists. In brief, it means all questions have to be answered in the affirmative on topics such as objectives and cost analysis before the U.S. would take military action. The doctrine is a great example of his vision, even though in many cases he couldn't persuade all the parts to fulfill the commitment to his ideas.

General Colin Powell was so invested in the idea of leadership that he laid out thirteen rules for it. They were posted on the State Department's website after his death in 2021.

Lessons

I took some general lessons away from what Powell said to me in those days in Tudor City, and they include:

- Character manifests itself through both word and deed.
- It's best to lead by example, and that example should be consistent.
- Leaders should be consistent but not stubborn.
- It's not only allowed but also vital to change your mind and your actions when the facts change.
- Your colleagues, staff, or friends know when you're being totally honest or bluffing. Don't bluff.
- Be optimistic but realistic. Find the aspects of a situation or problem that are promising and pursue them.
- A leader considers criticism but isn't cowed or overwhelmed by it.
- Self-doubt can be healthy when recognized and controlled.
- People yearn to be led but not bullied.
- Kindness, such as speaking someone's native language if you can, is the best icebreaker.
- Be visible. Don't sulk in your tent.
- Yelling rarely helps. Be firm but polite when dealing with employees, clients, or friends.

Valéry Giscard d'Estaing

> We have sown a seed. . . . Instead of a half-formed Europe,
> we have a Europe with a legal entity, with a single currency,
> common justice, a Europe which is about to have its own
> defense.
>
> —Valéry Giscard d'Estaing

Perhaps nothing in Valéry Giscard d'Estaing's long career in French, European, and international politics distinguished him more than his early and unfaltering embrace of the idea of Europe as an economic and political entity, including former Soviet bloc countries, now comprising the twenty-seven-member European Union. His political stances that led to this union displayed immense courage in the face of opposition from Gaullist nationalists and incredulousness from all sides of the political spectrum when he declared before the fall of the Soviet bloc in 1989 that Poland, Hungary, and the Czech Republic would join NATO before the end of the century. They did, in 1999.

It's likely Giscard took some of his inspiration from President Charles de Gaulle, who said: "A man of character finds a special attractiveness in difficulty, since it is only by coming to grips with difficulty that he can realize his potentialities."

Giscard was born a transnational European in Koblenz, Germany, in 1926, while his financier father was working there. He joined the French Resistance at age eighteen, and later the army, before attending the prestigious École Nationale d'Administration. He worked at various government jobs, was elected to the National Assembly in 1956, and at the age of thirty-six became de Gaulle's finance minister. It was during his second stint as finance minister, under President Georges Pompidou, that Giscard teamed up with his colleague Helmut Schmidt, then the German finance minister, to begin laying the framework for the European Monetary System. This led to the bloc's common currency, the euro, which replaced the franc, deutsche mark, lira, and other currencies.

Bear in mind that all of this happened in the relatively recent shadow of World War II, during which Germany occupied much of France; killed, arrested, and deported Jews, Roma, and Catholics, among others; and looted French museums and wineries. There was a growing consensus after the war that steps must be taken to ensure that the two nations, and indeed the Continent, never fight again.

Giscard had the political courage to fight for this ideal, even if the politics of the moment opposed it, usually based on French nationalism and a lasting mistrust in many quarters of the Germans. Giscard's boss, President de Gaulle, another man of immense character, who had beaten the Germans on the battlefield, wanted them subordinate but not oppressed. Germany, led by Schmidt's boss, Konrad Adenauer, another exemplar of character, wanted to tie the country to the West, not the nascent Soviet bloc in the East.

The relationship of Valéry Giscard d'Estaing and Helmut Schmidt dates from the 1960s, when each man worked in his country's finance ministry, and blossomed when they both became finance ministers and later president and chancellor, respectively. Their collaboration resulted in the European Monetary System, which evolved into the euro, and ensured stable, if occasionally rocky, relations between the two ex-combatant nations. During their frequent meetings, Giscard, who spoke little German, and Schmidt, who spoke little French, would dismiss their aides and speak in their common language: English. The two men grew so comfortable with each other that, reported Elizabeth Pond in the *Christian Science Monitor* in 1980, during a visit to Schmidt's house in Hamburg, the famously formal Giscard actually took off his suit coat. A spokesman was asked if he also took off his tie. "No one," the aide replied, "has ever seen Giscard without his tie."

I had various indirect and direct encounters with Giscard. On the day of his election victory over François Mitterrand in 1974 my wife, Jan, and I were staying in a lovely small *pensione* on the Riviera. I had no idea who Giscard was, but when we came down to pay the bill and check out, the owner was so thrilled her choice had won the election that she paid our bill for us, saying, "He will be great for France." I paid attention to Giscard after that.

On the subject of language, while fluent in English, as are all graduates of the École Nationale d'Administration, Giscard was elected in 2003 to a spot on the Académie Française, the ultimate guardian of the French language. I once saw him at a prestigious conference in Italy, where he spoke in French. Since nearly everyone at the conference spoke English as well as Italian, I asked him why he chose to speak in French. "Because I am French," he said matter-of-factly.

During his presidency from 1974 to 1981, Giscard helped modernize the postwar, rigidly Catholic France he inherited. Rules on abortion, contraception, and divorce were brought into line with those of most of the rest of Europe and North America. He pushed big ideas, such as spreading a high-speed train network that could whisk you to Bordeaux from Paris in about two hours, begun under his predecessor (the *train à grande vitesse*, or TGV); boosted France's reliance on nuclear power; and championed massive projects in Paris, including converting an old train station into the Musée d'Orsay and building a modern Arc de Triomphe (a massive hollow square) at La Défense on the western outskirts of the city.

Ultimately, a recession near the end of his term, as well as accusations that Giscard had benefited from the gift of two diamonds from an African dictator when he was finance minister (charges he always denied), led to his defeat in a rematch with Mitterrand in the 1981 election.

On May 20, 1981, Giscard and his cabinet met for the last time during his presidency, and he gave a televised speech to the nation during which he said *au revoir* (until next time) instead of *adieu* (goodbye) and pledged to remain at France's disposal. He then walked off screen, pointedly leaving an empty chair, implying to many who were watching that his longtime rival and successor, François Mitterrand, wasn't worthy of the seat. In 1986, however, Mitterrand won re-election, something that had eluded Giscard.

After his presidency, Giscard was reelected to the National Assembly and later the European Parliament, where he kept fighting for his European ideal. Even in defeat from the highest office in his country, he did not give up serving.

In 2001, he was appointed chairman of the Convention on the Future of the European Union, and he spent the next three years leading a group of 102 policymakers charged with writing a constitution that would supplement the Treaty of Rome, which founded the EU and which would strengthen the bloc's economic and political ties. To his regret, in 2005, a draft constitution that had been ratified by eighteen member states was rejected by French and Dutch voters and was never enacted.

When Giscard began his political career in the early 1960s, the European Union consisted of the six founding states: Belgium, France, Germany, Italy, Luxembourg, and the Netherlands. When he first became finance minister, there were nine members, the U.K., Denmark, and Ireland having joined in 1973.

During the final year of his presidency (1981), Greece joined, followed by Spain and Portugal in 1986. Austria, Finland, and Sweden joined in 1995. Between 2004 and 2013, thirteen more countries joined: the Czech Republic, Estonia, Cyprus, Latvia, Lithuania, Hungary, Malta, Poland, Slovakia, Slovenia, Romania, Bulgaria, and Croatia. Britain left in 2016, leaving twenty-seven members.

NATO expanded similarly, growing since 1949 from twelve to thirty-two members. The membership closely tracks that of the EU, plus the US and Canada.

Lessons

Here are some character lessons you can draw from the life and work of Valéry Giscard d'Estaing:

- Defeat strengthens character and can breed later triumph. Giscard did valuable work on European unity after his defeat in the 1981 French presidential election, remaining active in the French and European Parliaments, promoting the euro, and helping draft a European Constitution.
- Honesty and openness in relationships is a vital character trait and can produce unexpected results. Today's Europe would not be the same had Giscard not developed his very special relationship with Helmut Schmidt.
- Experience leads to insight. By keeping active in European affairs and frequently meeting other leaders, Giscard understood in the late 1980s that the Soviet Union couldn't survive as then constituted. By the time the Soviet bloc dissolved in 1989 he was virtually alone in predicting, correctly, that Poland, Hungary, and then-Czechoslovakia would join NATO by the end of the century.
- Formality can serve a purpose. While sometimes dismissed as haughty by Frenchmen and foreigners alike, Giscard remained widely respected until his death, at age ninety-four, in 2020. Nobody really expected him to take off his tie in public.

Muhammad Anwar Sadat

If you don't have the power to change yourself, then
nothing will change around you.

—Anwar Sadat

Leadership often involves changing a political stance without
it being completely clear that this action is either widely supported or of immediate benefit to those affected. To do this, a
leader has to show courage, persistence, and patience; to be per-
suasive; and to remain totally committed. In many cases, a particular political or military leader is uniquely suited to lead the
180-degreee change because of a previous opposing stance.
Think of President Richard Nixon going to "Red" China in
1972, a world-changing event.

Another such chain of events began with Egyptian president
Anwar Sadat's visit to Jerusalem in November 1977, during
which he addressed the Knesset, the Israeli parliament. This
visit precipitated negotiations leading to the Camp David accords the following year, a Nobel Peace Prize for Sadat and Israeli leader Menachim Begin, and a peace treaty in 1979 that is
still in effect today.

The Camp David Accords were two agreements signed by
Anwar Sadat and Israeli prime minister Menachem Begin on
September 17, 1978, under the watchful eye of President
Jimmy Carter, after seventeen days of secret negotiations at
the U.S. president's retreat in Maryland. The agreements,
which proved to be the diplomatic high point of Carter's
one-term presidency, led to a peace between Israel and
Egypt that endures to this day.

It may also be said that Sadat's leadership directly led to his
death. He was assassinated in 1981 by Islamic fundamentalists

outraged by the peace treaty with Israel, as well as his domestic crackdown on their movement. He thus joined political martyrs ranging from Mohandas Gandhi to Abraham Lincoln to John F. Kennedy to Martin Luther King Jr. to Indira Gandhi. It's worth reflecting on the character traits each of these individuals possessed.

Like Sadat, they were all identified with and committed to an idea, broadly, that everybody, regardless of race, religion, or political beliefs, deserves an equal chance in life, and it's a government's business to provide that. Throughout history this had proved easier said than done. Charismatic leaders from Julius Caesar to Adolf Hitler, who didn't possess the character traits of compassion, humility, or empathy, have led people astray, often with disastrous consequences.

Islamic fundamentalism developed in the early twentieth century as a backlash against Western secular ideas that were seen to be undercutting fundamental ideas expressed in the Koran for how Muslims should lead their lives. In religious terms it resembled Evangelical Christianity or Orthodox Judaism, but politically some of its adherents advocated and practiced violence against nonbelievers. In Egypt, the main fundamentalist group, the Society of the Muslim Brothers, also known as the Muslim Brotherhood, was founded by the scholar Hassan al-Banna in 1928. Outlawed off and on since then, the group preaches strict adherence to Sharia law as given in the Koran, which was written in the seventh century.

Members of another group, the Egyptian Islamic Jihad, killed Sadat in 1981. The Muslim Brotherhood has participated in politics, and its candidate, Mohamed Morsi, won the 2012 presidential election, but was overthrown a year later.

Anwar Sadat was born on December 25, 1918, just after the end of World War I. He was one of thirteen children in a poor family. He attended the Royal Military Academy and entered the Army in 1938. Along with Gamal Abdel Nasser, whom he would succeed as president, Sadat and others conspired to expel the British from Egypt and upend the Egyptian monarchy. He was imprisoned by the British during World War II, accused of, among other things, involvement in the assassination of Minister of Finance Amin Osman and being a spy for Nazi Germany. Sadat participated in the revolution that overthrew King Farouk in 1952, and in 1954 Nasser brought him into the new government. He eventually became vice president and in 1970 became president upon Nasser's death.

To the surprise of many, Sadat was able to consolidate his power and began a significant modernization of the Egyptian economy. He expelled the Russian military from the country and turned politically to the West. Less known is Sadat's outreach to many religious groups, including to Evangelical Christians and Catholics. He invited Billy Graham to visit Egypt in 1975 and Sadat visited Pope Paul VI in the Vatican in 1976.

But Sadat also encouraged the growth of Islamic fundamentalism, his ultimate undoing, believing it was a conservative movement, and joined with Syria in attacking Israeli forces in the Sinai Peninsula and Golan Heights in the Yom Kippur War of 1973.

But during the lengthy and arduous peace negotiations in 1978, his leadership was contagious: both Begin and Carter had to withstand withering criticism at home, but both could point to Sadat as a touchstone.

Another aspect of leadership is the ability to communicate, to get one's ideas across to target audiences. Sadat knew he needed U.S. support in his peace efforts, and he skillfully cultivated television journalists, especially Barbara Walters of ABC News. Walters had covered Sadat's visit to Israel and had gone to Egypt to interview him, and during a second visit to Israel to interview Prime Minister Menachem Begin, she learned that Begin had invited Sadat to join the interview, which turned out to be one of the most consequential of her career, coming just before Camp David. Walters had said Sadat was the interviewee she most admired.

In various speeches and recountings, Sadat reflected on his actions.

He said he made the trip to Jerusalem to pursue peace, even though this would be difficult and would take a long time and much effort. It needed to be done for future generations.

This is similar to the reasoning behind Nixon's trip to China, mentioned earlier, and falls well short of bragging because it is true. Leaders accept challenges, display vision and imagination, and enable their followers to look to the future. Was it a gamble? Sure. Was it a risky gamble? No. The trip was prepared well in advance. Attention to detail is another trait of a good leader.

This is another display of leadership, showing the courage it took to make that trip to Israel, but reminding Israel and the rest of the world that peace was not yet achieved. This statement is brutally honest, not cloaked in political or diplomatic nicety, and remember, it was being made in the den of the enemy. That takes courage.

But a real leader doesn't rest on his laurels, he moves forward. Sadat was determined to plow ahead, despite the obstacles, and he mourned all the victims of war and violence. While this may seem a bit disingenuous coming from the leader of the Egyptian side in the Yom Kippur War, it was clearly a genuine denunciation of war as the solution. Sadat led by placing peace in the Middle East in its broader context and bringing the horrors of war down to the human level.

The goal, he reiterated in his Nobel Peace Prize speech in 1978, "is to bring security to the peoples of the area, and the Palestinians in particular, restoring to them all their right to a life of liberty and dignity. . . . This is what I stand for."

He made his purpose clear but also implanted a moral component as he reminded his audience that the Palestinian issue had not been resolved. Tragically, it remains unresolved today, more than forty-five years later.

A true leader employs empathy and projection to bring audiences along and does not shy away from a moral compass, no matter how uncomfortable that may be to some.

Sadat once bravely reminded the Israeli Parliament that Palestinians have a right to life, liberty, and dignity, not a sentiment often heard in the Knesset then or now. Nobody applauded, but this wasn't an applause line. It was another aspect of the character trait of leadership. A leader speaks the truth even when it may not be convenient. But as Sadat did in his Nobel speech, try to be encompassing and empathetic.

He later said Egypt was deeply committed to peace. This shows again the confidence of a leader who is firm in his convictions and sure of his facts. He referenced history and faith. As we'll see later, character is often manifest by a knowledge of history and a deeply held faith. We'll see this in John McCain, Theodore Hesburgh, and others throughout this book.

While Sadat's leadership changed the relations between Egypt and Israel, restored the Sinai to Egypt, and prevented further wars between the countries, it never fully achieved the promise outlined above. In part this was because of his assassination in 1981 by fundamentalist army members, in part because Palestinian leadership wasn't as visionary as Sadat's.

Character and leadership as embodied by Anwar Sadat are sorely missing as I write this, with Israel and Hamas engaged in a vicious war. This isn't to suggest that all would be well in the Middle East if Sadat had survived longer, but it is reasonable to assume things would be better.

Character matters.

Lessons

Anwar Sadat's unique life offers several lessons on courage.

- If you're doing what you know to be the right thing, do it despite the consequences.
- Think big. Many things haven't been done because nobody's tried them before.

- Think beyond local boundaries. Many decisions and actions have implications well beyond the local.
- Be patient. The Camp David Accords took nearly two weeks of painstaking negotiations.
- Communicate. Leadership doesn't exist in a vacuum.
- Stick to your guns even when facing hostile audiences. Honesty and persuasion will win them over. So will empathy.

Mother Teresa

God still loves the world through you and through me.

—Mother Teresa

Mary Teresa Bojaxhiu, whose birth name was Anjezë Gonxhe Bojaxhiu but was known to the world as Mother Teresa, and later Saint Teresa of Calcutta after her 2016 canonization, was an Indian-Albanian nun who founded the Missionaries of Charity in 1950 and until her death in 1997 fed and succored the poor all over the world, raising millions in contributions but remaining faithful to her flock. The organization now comprises more than six thousand nuns in more than 133 countries.

Missionaries of Charity is one of millions of nongovernmental organizations around the world that supplement the work of governments and generally work with poor or underserved populations that need food, health care, shelter, or other services they can't get from their local governments. The term *nongovernmental organization* was introduced in article 71 of the United Nations Charter in 1945. Besides Mother Teresa's group, prominent NGOs include Save the Children, Doctors Without Borders, Amnesty International, and the Red Cross.

Mother Teresa demonstrated leadership by building a global organization from nothing while remaining firmly anchored to her religious beliefs. This was no mean feat for a poor Albanian nun. What carried her to fame was an unshakable, and evident, faith and a holy aura that later resulted in her sainthood.

Mother Teresa's speeches and homilies demonstrate her leadership traits.

She always asked God for the strength to make the right decisions. Her words are filled with unfailing optimism and calls for activism. Love instead of hatred. Forgiveness where there is wrong. Harmony in the place of discord. Truth in place of error. Faith instead of doubt. Hope overcoming despair. Light instead of shadows. Joy replacing sadness. She often used the call-and-response rhetoric of the church. The lessons are clear: Comfort others rather than seek comfort for yourself. Understand others even if you aren't understood. It's more important to love than to be loved. You needn't consciously seek your soul in order to find it. Forgive and you'll be forgiven. Death leads to eternal life.

Yes, this is pretty basic Catholicism, as espoused by Saint Francis, but it is also a powerful leadership message. If you can show people how to turn hatred into love, discord into harmony, error into truth, doubt into faith, despair into hope, darkness into light, and sadness into joy, they're going to follow you. We'll see this again when I talk about Theodore Hesburgh. But let me make clear that the faith that inspires religious leaders is a character trait. For them, and for many of you, I trust, it is the touchstone of the ideals that inspire others.

She preached that if you are self-effacing and true to yourself, you will help others beyond measure. That was Mother's Teresa's touchstone. It explains why she was a leader who attracted so many followers. Authenticity. WYSIWYG (though she would not have put it that way): what you see is what you get.

Even in the lofty spotlight of receiving the Nobel Peace Prize in 1979, her focus remained unwavering: "Our poor people are great people, are very lovable people, they don't need our pity and sympathy, they need our understanding love."

The poor were created by the same loving hand of God, she reminded everyone.

A powerful testament from an amazing woman, who led by doing and in so leading made a true difference. To her, leading by example was not only natural but holy. Can anyone read her words and not give to the local food bank or other charity? Or volunteer to help the less fortunate?

Mother Teresa was a leader who not only helped the poor but also understood their human dignity.

Why did this Albanian nun, among so many other religious humanitarians, capture the love and attention of the world and prompt the Catholic Church to recognize her as a saint?

To me the answer is character.

Mother Teresa's relationship to God was clearly the most important factor in her life. But it's important to identify what made her a leader: that the relationship motivated her to devote her life to helping others and inspire others to do the same. It wasn't sufficient just to believe. One also had to bring those beliefs to life.

Her life illustrates another aspect of character. Actions can very often be far more important than words. Nobody remembers all of what Mother Teresa said, but everyone knows what she did: She touched millions of followers by her dedication to the poor and disadvantaged. She showed how to actually help, rather than just offer thoughts and prayers. Though she fervently believed in the power of prayer, it was her actions that inspired her followers to devote their lives to helping others. She was a model for us all.

Character can change lives.

Lessons

While none of us is likely to be canonized a saint, we can learn from Mother Teresa's life and works.

- Don't allow any space between what you do and what you say. People will follow your actions and will know immediately if your words don't match them.
- Use your faith. It is not just thoughts or words.
- Leaders come in all shapes and sizes. And they aren't all generals or presidents.

Dwight D. Eisenhower

In the councils of government, we must guard against the acquisition of unwanted influence, whether sought or unsought, by the military-industrial complex.
　　—Dwight D. Eisenhower, farewell address to the nation,
January 17, 1961

Whether as commander of the D-Day invasion, key to the liberation of Europe in World War II, or as the thirty-fourth president of the United States, Dwight David Eisenhower was above all a leader. He not only warned about the outsize influence of the military-industrial complex but also laid the foundations for the space program and helped create the U.S. interstate highway system that was eventually named for him. He was never flashy but was always effective, a classic character trait of the true leader.

To me, Dwight Eisenhower, generally known as Ike, was one of our best and underrated presidents, aside from his heroism and leadership in World War II. If the times are any reflection of their leaders, then his steady hand on the helm during the 1950s ushered in the postwar boom and reverberates to our day. We have much to thank Ike for and much to learn from him.

Eisenhower was born in 1890 in Denison, Texas, and raised in Abilene, Kansas, in a large family of Mennonite Christians. He graduated from the West Point military academy in 1915, ranking about the middle of his class. He wanted to fight in

Europe in World War I but instead was assigned to a tank training unit at home. Between the wars he proceeded steadily up
the Army ranks and became a brigadier general in 1941, just before America entered the war after the attack on Pearl Harbor.

During the war Eisenhower quickly assumed key leadership
roles, commanding Operation Torch, the invasion of North
Africa through Tunisia, and the capture of Sicily, which ultimately toppled Mussolini. His ultimate challenge was Operation Overlord, the June 6, 1944, Allied landings on the beaches
of Normandy after crossing from England. The daring D-Day
landings eventually liberated France. After the decisive Battle of
the Bulge turned back a German counterattack in early 1945,
and the Soviets captured Berlin that spring, Germany surren-
dered, on May 7, 1945. Toward the end of the war, Ike was
promoted to general of the Army, the highest rank.

Operation Overlord was so risky that Eisenhower, as Supreme Allied Commander, prepared a letter to be released
in the event the landings failed.

He said his decision to attack was based on the best information possible, but took complete responsibility for what-
could be a "failure." Ike also praised the troops, the Army
Air Corps, and the Navy for their bravery and devotion to
duty and country.

Of course, while the cost in manpower was huge, the plan
proved to be the right one, and the war was won. But let's
consider that thankfully never-delivered message. Eisenhower had plenty of advice, much of it contradictory, from
his French, British, and Soviet allies, including de Gaulle and
Churchill, on when and where to launch his attack on German-
occupied territory. There was also plenty of advice from his
own generals, including George Marshall.

Some of these discussions leaked—in some cases intentionally—to throw off the Germans, but much disagreement

was real. Eisenhower made the final decisions, and he's saying that if he got it wrong, nobody was to blame but himself, not flawed advice. That's the essence of leadership and character. When things go well, thank everyone who helped; when things go south, take the blame yourself.

After the German surrender, Eisenhower stayed in Europe to oversee the American part of occupied Germany, was later chief of staff of the Army, and become president of Columbia University in New York, and then the supreme NATO commander. From this post, he ran successfully for president as a Republican in 1952 and was reelected in 1956.

Eisenhower's leadership abilities were evident in each post he held. The military roles required courage, tenacity, and the ability to motivate others. The presidency also required a leader who could inspire, decide on a course for the nation, and lead political and social society along that course. While history may regard his presidency as somewhat uneventful and in fact somewhat boring, he accomplished or laid the groundwork for much of today's economy. We all rely on the interstate highway system, the internet, which was largely invented by DARPA (the federal Defense Advanced Research Projects Agency), the GPS system of satellites, and much more. Sometimes boring but effective is the way to go.

The U.S. owes the system of highways that crisscross the country from east to west and north to south, and indeed a big chunk of our current prosperity, to Dwight D. Eisenhower. Having seen how difficult it was to move U.S. troops around the country between the wars, and having seen the German autobahns during the war, Eisenhower championed a stalled plan to create an interstate highway system. It now comprises nearly fifty thousand miles of highway and would probably cost north of $500 billion to build today. He initially backed it as a key military objective during the Cold War, but today the system moves people, goods, and produce around the country freely, and was both a contributor to and facilitator of the postwar economic boom. The roads that bear even numbers, such as Interstate 80, run east and west. The roads with odd numbers, such as Interstate 95, run north and south. Its formal name is the Dwight D. Eisenhower System of Interstate and Defense Highways. It's one of the few man-made structures on Earth that can be seen by the naked eye from space.

One of Eisenhower's greatest challenges after the war was the economic, political, and scientific competition with the Soviet Union, our ally turned rival for the hearts and minds of the world. This Cold War would continue until the dissolution of the Soviet bloc in 1989. Berlin had been divided between East and West and the Soviets would erect the Berlin Wall just after Ike left office. Meanwhile, sports and scientific rivalry grew, and in the late 1950s the Soviets seemed ahead.

The world was shocked on October 4, 1957, when the Soviet Union launched Sputnik, the first satellite to orbit the earth. So profound was the sense that the U.S. was falling behind the Soviets (despite Eisenhower's initial dismissal of Sputnik as just a little ball) that the U.S. only four months later launched the Advanced Research Projects Agency (later the Defense Advanced Research Projects Agency, or DARPA). Months later, the National Aeronautics and Space Administration, or NASA, was established, and Eisenhower's successor, John F. Kennedy, would pledge to put a man on the moon and would do so a few months after Eisenhower's death. In April 1961 Yuri Gagarin became the first human to orbit the Earth, a feat the U.S. would accomplish the following year. For his part, Eisenhower was skeptical about spending billions on the space program, but he created the agencies that did just that.

In office, Eisenhower believed in using the relatively new medium of television to stay in touch with the public. He held the first televised press conference in 1955 and went on to hold a total of nearly two hundred, by far more than any of his recent successors.

His two terms encompassed the rise and fall of Senator Joseph McCarthy's campaign to root out perceived Communist infiltration of the State Department and Army. While Eisenhower said little in public in order not to give McCarthy political oxygen, he did respond to McCarthy's attempts to investigate White House staff by adopting the doctrine of executive privilege, which had not existed previously. This effectively blunted the probes.

Eisenhower also used his time in the White House to implement the integration of the armed forces begun by Harry Truman, and to propose the Civil Rights Acts of 1957 and 1960. In 1957, he federalized the Arkansas National Guard in order to enforce desegregation of the Little Rock schools, in defiance of the state's governor. While Lyndon Johnson later expanded civil rights legislation, Eisenhower played a key role in trying to ensure fair treatment of all citizens.

No one is perfect. Ike was famous for his temper, so much so that his staff dubbed him the "terrible-tempered Mr. Bang," but he used self-discipline to curb that tendency.

Most of all, he was trusted—by the troops he led in war and the citizens he led in peace. Like Colin Powell, Eisenhower exuded optimism.

He is perhaps best remembered for two speeches, the so-called Chance for Peace speech in 1953, in which he warned of increased defense spending, and his farewell address in 1961, in which he warned of the dangers of the military-industrial complex. Both of these speeches reflected Eisenhower's distaste for government spending, though it should be noted that defense spending, largely aimed at the Soviet Union, rose by a lot during his two terms. In the first speech, delivered to the American Society of Newspaper Editors in Washington, DC, and televised, he said: "Every gun that is made, every warship launched, every rocket fired signifies, in the final sense, theft from those who hunger and are not fed, those who are cold and not clothed. . . . This is not a way of life at all, in any true sense. Under the cloud of threatening war, this is humanity hanging from a cross of iron."

What a remarkable speech, not just from the country's greatest war hero, but also from a pro-defense Republican. Sure, times were different, but it took great determination and character for Eisenhower to explain to the American people the choices they faced and the consequences of putting tax dollars into military hardware.

In his final speech as president, Eisenhower seemed to have given up trying to rein in defense spending. He pointed out that previously the country had no large arms makers but rather companies that turned their domestic production to wartime production when needed, and then turned back. But after World War II, giant defense companies sprung up, making arms in peacetime.

In addition, nearly three million people—at the time an unheard-of figure—were making a living off the military, either as soldiers or suppliers.

The military-industrial complex, he warned, threatened the very structure of society, and people needed to pay attention. Security and liberty should prosper together.

Again, a remarkable speech from a soldier, but now a statesman whose job it had been to bring justice and prosperity to his nation. He knew better than anyone that you can't have guns and butter at levels that would satisfy the military and the general populace. His Republicanism involved choices, and right then the country needed more butter.

Think of the self-confidence and strength of character that enabled Ike to give both of these speeches at the start and end of his presidency.

Leadership is speaking the truth.

Lessons

Dwight Eisenhower led as a soldier and politician through the quality and transparency of his actions.

- Great leaders aren't necessarily flashy, but an air of quiet authority makes them effective.
- Slow and steady wins the race.
- The character of leaders and commanders is what inspires respect and trust.
- No one is perfect. Know your weakness and work to overcome or at least limit it.
- Hard truths need to be stated firmly and calmly, backed by facts.

Chapter Three

INNOVATION

I have not failed 10,000 times—I've successfully found 10,000 ways that will not work.

—Thomas Edison

The doggedness, optimism, and confidence that propelled Thomas Edison to keep looking for that 10,001st way that *would* work are the character traits that drive the most successful inventors, researchers, and creators. But that's not to say that everybody who is confident and stubborn will invent the iPhone or discover insulin or create Mickey Mouse. As we look at the lives and careers of Steve Jobs, Frederick Banting, and Walt Disney, bear in mind the additional spark of genius each of these men possessed. But without the character traits that are within everyone's grasp, their genius wouldn't have emerged.

Innovation is fed by curiosity, ingenuity, flexibility, and determination. It's also usually an outcome of sheer hard work. Think of Edison's ten thousand failures. And if sometimes a discovery or an innovation seems to be the result of luck, recall a saying usually attributed to South African golfer Gary Player: "The harder I practice, the luckier I get."

Innovators may seem to be unicorn-like creatures that pop up in the world from time to time. Sometimes it seems that either you are an innovator or you're not—that geniuses are found rarely and genius can't be trained. You must be born with it.

But that's not true of most innovators. Steve Jobs did see the world—particularly the world of product possibility and design—differently than the thousands of other Silicon Valley entrepreneurs of the 1970s. He was gifted but far from unique. What set him apart was determination. Frederick Banting was a mid-level medical researcher when his insights led him to discover insulin as a treatment for diabetes. His character prompted him to offer it to the world for one dollar. Walt Disney was one of dozens of artists producing animated films in Hollywood in the 1920s. It didn't take a genius to draw Mickey Mouse, but it did take a determined, grounded, innovative entrepreneur to build the Magic Kingdom that the Disney Company became.

Steve Jobs

Innovation distinguishes between a leader and a follower.
—Steve Jobs

Innovations for which Steve Jobs was directly or indirectly responsible changed the world in the twentieth and twenty-first centuries: the Apple II, the iPad, the iPod, the Macintosh, Air-Pods, the MacBook, and of course the iPhone. Now a staple in nearly everyone's pocket, the iPhone or its competitors, the lit-tle plastic brick that is at once a telephone, camera, television, radio, stereo, GPS, calculator, and internet interface was a total surprise to the audience when Jobs unveiled the first one in 2007.

It was a product that changed everything. In introducing the new concept, he repeated over and over: Apple is introducing an iPod music player with touch controls, a phone, and an internet-access device. iPod, phone, internet. A few in the audience began to get it and started applauding. iPod, phone, internet. A few delighted shouts. He wasn't talking about three devices—it was all in one, the iPhone. The audience, at first stunned, then stood and cheered.

It's useful to remember that this was not even two decades ago, yet devices of the kind that Jobs unveiled are now ubiquitous.

Innovators really do change the world, often by exhibiting the character and focus that set them apart as much as their genius.

Steve Jobs had focus. The importance of this trait is often underappreciated. His longtime chief designer, Sir Jony Ive, recently recalled Jobs as "the most remarkably focused person" he had ever met. By that, he meant that Jobs had the discipline to say no to a good idea because he needed to focus on something else. He didn't let himself get scattered.

That's an often-overlooked character trait—the ability and confidence to say no when you're sure that everyone around you saying yes is wrong, or when you think saying yes to an extraneous idea or request will interrupt your work or concentration. Do it gracefully and you won't be thought of as aloof or arrogant. But be absolutely sure your confidence is well grounded.

Jobs's focus undoubtedly led to the stream of products listed above, but it also left him open to criticism, often justified, that he was hard on coworkers and employees. He certainly didn't suffer fools, and he was famously distrustful of the press, with the Apple press relations department being one of the least cooperative of all the tech companies.

Jobs had a famous rivalry, at least in the view of the technology press, with Microsoft founder Bill Gates. Gates tended to do more personal appearances and attend more conferences and appear on TV more frequently than did Jobs.

In 1983, a very young Jobs invited a very young Gates to an early Apple conference, where they played a version of the then-popular Dating Game, in which Jobs quizzed software makers, including Gates, on what they liked about Apple and how they might collaborate. Gates played along.

Nearly twenty-five years later, in 2007, after years of separately attending the D: All Things Digital conference produced by the *Wall Street Journal*—if Gates was to speak at dinner, Jobs would speak at breakfast the next day, or vice versa—they finally agreed to share a stage to be interviewed by *WSJ* journalists Walt Mossberg and Kara Swisher.

Jobs, in his signature blue jeans and black mock turtleneck, answered the first question—what has the other guy contributed to their industry—with a gracious tribute to Microsoft's software. Gates returned the favor, praising Apple's computers, and the evening became a master class in the history of the tech industry as told by two of its creators. This event is available on YouTube and well worth watching.

Recovered from his first bout with the cancer that would ultimately kill him in 2011, Jobs gave a remarkable commencement address at Stanford in 2005. In it, he discussed many of the traits that made up his character.

He started by saying he never went to college, much less attended a graduation. He showed disarming honesty while pointing out indirectly that you can do great things without a formal education.

You can see that honesty and a measure of humility are important character traits.

Jobs then told the story of dropping out of Reed College after six months, but dropping in on various classes for the next eighteen months. In particular, he dropped in on a calligraphy class and learned about various typefaces and typography. He said if he hadn't chanced on this course, he might never have been able to conceive and design, or help design, the various Apple products we all now take for granted.

This is an important reminder that everything matters in the shaping of one's character, even events that may seem unrelated or a detour. Experiences and incidents all add up, manifesting themselves eventually in how we make the choices we make and what we can achieve. As with the butcher who manages to use every part of the pig except the squeak, everything matters.

Steve Jobs's time-passing calligraphy course ultimately changed the direction of modern computer design.

Jobs was a great believer in connecting the dots, a process that works only retrospectively to what you've seen or heard or observed, sometimes without knowing you're doing so. One idea leads to another, even after many years. You've got to trust your gut instincts.

So, is the ability to connect the dots a character trait? Not on the surface, but it does reflect vision and curiosity, which are. And Jobs's point about trusting your gut is a vital one. Virtually every story in this book is about a person who had the strength of character to trust their instincts, be it about fighting a war or uniting Europe or leading a basketball team.

Jobs's next story is about how failing can lead to success, as was true with Thomas Edison and others. He told of being fired from Apple at age thirty, a year after the company had released the revolutionary Macintosh computer. He was tactful enough not to call that one of the most boneheaded business decisions ever made, but it was.

What happened was that in 1983 the Apple board had brought on John Sculley from Pepsi-Cola to be Jobs's boss. Sculley, a seasoned executive, was supposed to rein in the supposedly hot-headed Jobs. They got along pretty well but eventually clashed over policies, including software licensing and retail stores, and the board fired Jobs in 1985.

Jobs was understandably bitter, asking how the founder of a thriving company could get fired by its board, but he managed to channel that anger into creativity. Drawing on the strength of his character, he founded a computer maker called NeXT, which developed hardware and software that was later incorporated into many Apple products, especially its core operating system. Sculley left Apple in 1993 and Apple bought NeXT and, in effect, Jobs in 1997.

Let's reflect on this a minute. Turning defeat into victory is one of the common threads of this book and a key reflection of character. We'll see it in the chapters on Frederick Banting, Nelson Mandela, and Václav Havel, among others.

Don't get mad, get even is a useful if two-edged concept. The point is not to inflict the same outrage on your enemy that they inflicted on you, but rather to prove you were right and they were wrong by achieving your goals. That's pretty much what Jobs did, and his return to the company ushered in the golden years of Apple, leading up to the truly revolutionary introduction of the iPhone ten years after his return.

There are an estimated 1.5 billion iPhone users in the world. That's nearly a fifth of everyone on the planet, and that's not counting users of other types of smartphones that owe their existence to the iPhone. Talk about getting even.

Jobs later reflected that, like the serendipity of sitting in on that calligraphy class at Reed, getting fired was one of the best things that ever happened to him. In addition to NeXT, during his exile from Apple he started Pixar, the hugely successful animation studio that produced *Toy Story* and *Cars* among many other hits.

Jobs would later say that what he learned from his firing was to never give up and to do what you love to do, that burdens were lifted from his shoulders and he was freed from corporate responsibilities to just create. But that understates the importance of having the character to know you are right and to keep going, rather than withdraw into a cocoon of self-pity and just give up. As we've seen and will see again, the ability to not be bowed down by failure or mistakes but rather to learn from them is a key aspect of an admirable character.

It's also important, he later said, to not settle for just any job or opportunity that shows up after adversity hits. You need to think about what you really love to do and do that. Don't settle for just anything.

Not settling is another character trait too often confused with arrogance or stubbornness. It is neither. It's perhaps better defined as persistence, and it's something all the people profiled in this book share.

Jobs fought valiantly against the pancreatic cancer that eventually killed him. The disease spurred him to keep working as hard and as well as he could, knowing that his remaining time was limited.

In his Stanford commencement speech, he closed by citing the words of Stewart Brand, creator of the *Whole Earth Catalog*. On the back cover of the final issue was the photograph of a country road in the early morning with these words below: "Stay hungry. Stay foolish."

Jobs said he had always wished that for himself, and now wished it for the new graduates. Stay hungry. Stay foolish.

In 2010, near the end of his life, Jobs sent himself an email, released by his wife after his death. He remarked that he grew little of the food that he ate.

The great innovator went on to list all the things he enjoyed, from freedom to music and so on, which he did not have a hand in creating. He appreciated his fellow human beings.

The email said, appropriately, at the end: "Sent from my iPad," which of course he did give to the world.

What a powerful reminder that innovators owe much to those who came before, and as Newton said, "If I have seen further than others, it is by standing on the shoulders of giants."

Jobs stayed hungry for new ideas and was "foolish" enough to pursue those ideas even when others scoffed. Cancer took him far too soon, and likely deprived the world of many other innovations.

Lessons

Steve Jobs didn't just change our world through the products he unleashed at Apple; his too-short life offers a number of lessons.

- Connect the dots. Reflect on what has happened in your life that got you where you are, and how you can use that knowledge to make the most of your future.

- Learn to say no when saying yes would lead you down a false path or distract you from what you are concentrating on. Do it gracefully,
- Don't settle. Stay hungry. Stay foolish. These are simple ideas but very hard to integrate into our lives. School, work, parents, friends all seem to have rules that stifle creativity. The line between bending and breaking these rules—asserting your individuality without hurting others or yourself—can be a fine one.
- Don't lose faith. If you've done the research, experiments, field-testing, polling, fact-checking, or whatever convinces you that your ideas are worth pursuing, take any setbacks as motivation to get up and try again. The world may have written off Jobs when he was fired from Apple, but he never wrote himself off.

Frederick Banting

Insulin does not belong to me. It belongs to the world.
—Frederick Banting

It didn't exactly come to him in a dream, but after waking from a restless night on October 31, 1920, after having read a scientific journal article on the pancreas, Frederick Banting wrote down: "Diabetes Ligate pancreatic ducts of dog. Keep dog alive till acini degenerate leaving Islets. Try to isolate the internal secretion of these to relieve glycosuria." In other words, extract from the pancreases of dogs the hormone insulin, which diabetics lack to help them make glucose to fuel their bodies.

Pursuing this idea with colleague Charles Best in the laboratory of J. J. R. Macleod in Toronto, Banting and his team managed to isolate and extract insulin in 1921 and, with the help of Dr. James Collip, refine it enough to begin clinical trials on diabetic animals and humans the next year.

In the years prior to this breakthrough, diabetics either died quickly or were put on starvation diets that slowed the disease but eventually led to death anyway.

Banting and Macleod won the Nobel Prize in Physiology or Medicine in 1923. Banting shared his prize with Best. Macleod shared his prize with Collip.

Perhaps the best-known type 1 diabetic of the twentieth century was the actress Mary Tyler Moore, who raised millions of dollars for the Juvenile Diabetes Research Foundation. She published a book on her life with the disease, *Growing Up Again: Life, Loves, and Oh Yeah, Diabetes* (St. Martin's Press, 2009). Ms. Moore died at age eighty in 2017. Other well-known type 1 diabetics include former British prime minister Theresa May, U.S. Supreme Court justice Sonia Sotomayor, and actress Halle Berry.

Frederick Banting was born in 1891 in Ontario, Canada, studied divinity and then medicine at the University of Toronto, and served in the Canadian Army medical corps in World War I. He was wounded in 1918 and returned to Canada when the war ended. While working in general practice and teaching in Toronto, he became interested in diabetes, especially as it affected children.

Insulin had recently been identified as the hormone whose lack in the body caused the debilitating effects of diabetes.

The journal article Banting read was by Moses Barron, who noted that the pancreas deteriorated when it was blocked by gallstones as well as when its main duct was tied off. It occurred to him that by tying off the duct he'd be able to extract pure insulin-containing islet cells.

He began working on this in 1921 in Macleod's laboratory at the University of Toronto with Best. They tied off the pancreatic ducts in some dogs, waited seven weeks, then extracted the pancreases. They extracted the islet cells, gave them to diabetic dogs, and noticed a quick return to normal blood-sugar levels.

Banting and team's discovery of insulin came only after many, many failed experiments and, to his distress, a lot of dead animals. Banting, by all accounts, was a quiet, low-key, hard-graft scientist who used failure to keep trying and trying and trying. He wasn't a media star. Nor was he particularly well treated by his superiors.

Scientists often face roadblocks to research breakthroughs. Albert Einstein famously worked as a clerk at the patent office in Bern, Switzerland, until his three seminal papers on electromagnetism and gravity were published in 1905. More recently, Dr. Katalin Karikó persevered in her research on mRNA, which led to vaccines for AIDS, COVID, and other diseases, despite having her work ridiculed and being demoted at three major U.S. universities. With Drew Weissman, she won the Nobel Prize in Physiology or Medicine in 2023.

Dozens of Banting's experiments didn't work or worked poorly. That just made the team work harder. Eventually, they felt confident enough to start human trials. This meant more trial and error, trying to administer just the right amount of insulin to turn the body's intake of carbohydrates into energy, to counteract the buildup of sugar in the blood.

They tried various numbers of insulin shots throughout the day, before or after or in between meals. They tried administering it before or after exercise. They carefully measured the blood-sugar content of many patients' urine, to see what amount and timing led to the disappearance of excess blood sugar. They carefully adjusted dosage levels. They tried big doses and small doses at various times of the day, testing the urine each time.

They carefully measured and adjusted how many carbohydrates a patient was ingesting.

What's remarkable about this is how little treatment for type 1 diabetes has changed in the one hundred years since Banting's discovery. Yes, continuous glucose monitors have made both urine and finger-prick blood tests obsolete, and insulin pumps can in some cases replace needles and syringes. Much insulin is now man-made, but some still comes from the pancreases of pigs or cows. The principle is the same: Measure and treat with insulin or carbohydrates high or low blood glucose levels.

Even in Banting's day, the results were immediate and dramatic, prompting him to say in 1923 that all diabetics should be admitted to a hospital to receive instruction on how to care for their disease. The instruction included learning about their diet and tests for sugar and acetone in their urine to determine whether insulin is needed.

He noted that of 130 children who were given insulin, 120 were still living. However, of the 164 who did not receive insulin treatment, all but 12 had died.

Banting concluded that insulin was a treatment for diabetes, not a cure. It enables the burning of sufficient carbohydrates so that proteins and fats could be added to the diet to "provide energy for the economic burdens of life."

It works! Famous actresses, a Supreme Court justice, countless athletes, and hundreds of millions of ordinary people have found "energy for the economic burdens of life" through their insulin shots.

Banting famously said that "insulin doesn't belong to me, it belongs to the world," and in 1923, Banting, Best, and Collip were awarded the U.S. patents for insulin and sold them to the University of Toronto for one dollar. Eventually Eli Lilly and Company started producing insulin under a contract with the university.

Banting would be shocked by the current debate over the price of insulin in the United States. It costs about ten dollars to make a vial of insulin, but its retail cost can be ten times that. The U.S. government has capped insulin costs at thirty-five dollars a month for seniors on Medicare, with political pressure growing to extend that to everyone.

Banting later turned his research interests to cancer and other ailments. He was knighted in 1934 and during World War II he served as a liaison between North American and British doctors seeking treatments for chemical warfare injuries.

His mantra: "I am a firm believer in the theory that you can do or be anything you wish in this world, within reason, if you are prepared to make the sacrifices, think and work hard enough and long enough."

It's impossible to calculate how many lives were saved by Banting's persistence in developing ways to provide insulin to diabetics, but the number is surely in the millions. He should also be remembered for his desire to give insulin to the world without personal monetary enrichment.

One lesson for character here is that you don't have to make millions of dollars to contribute or to be life-changing. We saw this in Mother Teresa and her work to heal the spirit, and the same is true of thousands of selfless scientists like Frederick Banting whose lives are dedicated to healing the body.

Lessons

Frederick Banting made one of the great discoveries in medicine, and how he did it and what happened next offer valuable lessons.

- Inspiration can come at any time, even after a bad night's sleep. When it does, jump on it.
- Many experiments or marketing ideas or new product trials fail. Success often comes from repeated failure.
- Unselfishness is a powerful character trait. Banting wanted to share insulin with those who needed it without thought of profit.

- Always spread around credit. When the Nobel Prize committee didn't recognize his colleague Charles Best, Banting did, sharing the prize with him.

Walt Disney

All our dreams can come true if we have the courage to pursue them.

—Walt Disney

The innovations Walt Disney introduced in animated film-making and amusement parks transformed the entertainment industry in ways that are still playing out. Walt, who died in 1966, likely wouldn't have imagined that the company that bears his name would now encompass more than two hundred companies, including Pixar (*Toy Story*), Marvel (*X-Men*), Lucasfilm (*Star Wars*), National Geographic, ABC, ESPN, and twelve Disney theme parks!

It all started in 1923 when Walt and his brother Roy founded Disney Brothers Cartoon Studio. The first production, *Oswald the Lucky Rabbit*, a 1927 silent film, shows a skating rabbit that looks a lot like a long-eared Mickey Mouse. Mickey himself debuted in the company's first cartoon with synchronized sound, *Steamboat Willie*, the following year.

From *Steamboat Willie* through the Thunderbirds to today's CGI superhero epic, animation has come a long way. After Disney, Steve Jobs's Pixar (see page 42) and George Lucas's Star Wars franchises made animation ever more sophisticated. As noted, Disney now owns both Pixar and Lucasfilm. Walt Disney thought animation was magic, and he wasn't wrong. He saw it as a blend of visual entertainment and storytelling, offering pleasure and information to anyone throughout the world. "Animation can explain whatever the mind of man can conceive," he once said. "This facility makes it the most versatile and explicit means of communication yet devised for quick mass appreciation."

Throughout his career, Walt Disney was not only an inspired creator and innovator but also a shrewd businessman. He had the instinct to create lovable characters and adaptations of beloved fairy tales and later appealing theme parks that would delight not only children but also adults. A BBC TV interviewer once asked Disney if he designed his Mickey Mouse films for kids. "Well, no," he said. "You had to appeal to the adult. The adults had the money."

Actually, Disney thought he could appeal to everyone. And that is because he thought every adult had a child within. He wanted his movies to reach that forgotten spot and elevate it to awareness.

Innovators usually think well beyond their initial ideas to conjure up the widest possible applications. Disney created cartoons and amusement park rides as important ways to appeal to that child in everyone.

That's another great character lesson: Innovators never stop with just the original idea. They add, modify, and adapt all angles.

As the company grew and diversified, Disney knew he had to stay grounded, another character trait worth thinking about. "Our only hope is we never lose sight of one thing: that it was all started by a mouse," he said.

When Disney first introduced its version of animatronics, a life-size figure of Abraham Lincoln at the 1964 New York World's Fair, critics scoffed at the somewhat jerky delivery of the awkward figure. But Disney constantly worked on improving the technology, and now a much more lifelike Abe has his own space at Disneyland. The same thing happened to the dancing and singing dolls in It's a Small World, now a fixture at all the Disney parks. Today, Disney and other theme parks routinely use animatronic figures on their rides, ranging from pirates to bears to princesses.

As with animatronics and various other slow-to-develop ideas, Disney didn't always have a smooth path. But he never gave up. He considered that adversity in his life served to strengthen him. You may not always realize at the time, though, that getting knocked down may be the best thing that could have happened to you. Again, a prominent character trait of innovators and entrepreneurs: Take lessons from every circumstance, even those that may at first seem like setbacks. (We saw this lesson with Steve Jobs.)

Disney films were always wholesome, but they also usually contained an evil character, from Cruella de Vil in *101 Dalmatians* to Ursula in *The Little Mermaid*. Many Disney films featured witches.

Disney thought a lot about what children needed to understand the world. He did not ignore the "shadows" of existence. Children know they are there, and if adults never talk about them or show how to deal with them, children can become more afraid. They need to learn how to cope.

Trying to shield children from reality does them no favor. What is important, he said, is to teach them that good will triumph over evil. That is what he aimed to do in his movies.

This is another character trait to bear in mind: honesty and a sense of reality about what the world is like. Pretending everything is sweetness and light is insincere and is always found out. Trust is lost.

There is much to reflect on here. Character shows up early

in the child who is "sensitive, humorous, open-minded, eager to learn, and has a strong sense of excitement, energy, and healthy curiosity about the world," Disney noted. Those are all the right character traits to carry into adulthood, but many of us are not so lucky. Why not? To Disney, one of the reasons was that adults were too heavy-handed with children. Lecturing doesn't work to build character. Better to keep children interested in everything, to cultivate a love of learning. This philosophy can now be found in virtually every parenting book on the market.

If we think about it, pretty much everything Walt Disney turned his hand to was in aid of keeping children—and adults—interested. From lively animated cartoons to thrilling and charming amusement park rides to a talking Abraham Lincoln, everything Disney did had a positive, entertaining sheen.

Toward the end of his life, Disney reflected that a person should set goals early and then devote energy to reaching them. But even if that path should lead somewhere else, know—truly feel—that you have been alive.

Much like the animation industry he pioneered, Walt Disney would probably be astonished at the growth of the theme park industry. The first Disneyland opened in Anaheim, California, in 1955, arguably the second major theme park in the U.S., following Santa Claus Land in Indiana, which opened in 1946 (and which itself followed on a long tradition of fairs and mechanical rides). I remember at a meeting with Walt Disney long ago in California, he said he wanted to open a second park, after the Anaheim Disneyland, in Florida. Most of his audience shouted him down, saying it would never work. I just said: "It's a lot warmer in Florida than here, Walt." The Florida parks have been great successes. Since then, Disney itself added eleven parks in Florida, France, Hong Kong, and mainland China, as well as add-ons such as EPCOT (an idea of Walt's for an Experimental Prototype

Community of Tomorrow), which never fully came off. Competitors such as NBC's Universal Studios, with six parks, and Time-Warner's Six Flags, with twenty-seven parks, all sprang from Walt's original 1955 idea.

The Disney legacy is amazing, from a mouse to a Space Mountain. As Walt once said, "It's kind of fun to do the impossible."

Lessons

Walt Disney created some of the best-loved characters in entertainment, and then grew his company into a global empire. His life has many lessons.

- Innovation requires both inspiration and insight, of the kind that Disney displayed when inventing all those characters and knowing that he was marketing to the adults who wanted wholesome entertainment for their children and for themselves.
- Set your imagination free. Steamboat Willie to Sleeping Beauty's castle to Luke Skywalker.
- Learn from your mistakes. When kicked in the teeth, get back up and keep fighting.
- Never hector, lecture, or talk down to kids. Let them love to learn and to grow. Don't shield them; instead show them that good can win over evil.
- Be aware of what has influenced your decisions and stay humble and grounded. "It all started with a mouse."

Chapter Four

RESILIENCE

Character consists of what you do on the third and fourth
tries.

— James A. Michener

In your life, you will be confronted with many challenges, which
hopefully you can face by summoning your inner strength. This
inner strength is the character trait known as resilience, and as
the novelist James Michener says, it often manifests itself as the
refusal to give up when confronting a setback, much like we saw
in the previous chapter with Thomas Edison's ten thousand failures.

Resilience also allows people of character to withstand years
in prison because of their political beliefs, as was the case with
Nelson Mandela, Václav Havel, and Emmeline Pankhurst, or to
overcome the failure of one's body and change the world with
your mind, as did Stephen Hawking. And in Hawking's case,
resilience also meant adapting his theories when facts proved he
might have erred. For Mandela and Havel, resilience enabled
them to leave their prison cells and inspire and win the confidence and votes of their people and become presidents of their
countries. In Susan B. Anthony's and Pankhurst's cases, it
meant securing the right to vote for half the population of the
U.S. and U.K.—women.

We are all tested in life, some of us infrequently and some of us daily, whether by a difficult family or financial situation, illness, or just plain bad luck. Resilience is what allows us to fight back, to keep going.

Resilience doesn't mean acceptance. In fact, it's just the opposite. It's an ability to endure and emerge stronger from an ordeal. It requires a character that is courageous and self-assured.

We all need to be resilient from time to time. The profiles in this chapter will give you some of the tools you need to survive and bounce back.

Nelson Mandela

> Do not judge me by my successes. Judge me by how many times I fell down and got back up again.
>
> —Nelson Mandela

Nelson Mandela spent twenty-seven years in South African prisons before he was freed in 1990. He resumed his political career, and was elected president of South Africa in 1994, a year after he and F. W. de Klerk, his predecessor as president, were awarded the Nobel Peace Prize. During his presidency he established a truth and reconciliation commission to ensure a peaceful transition from apartheid. It was presided over by fellow Nobel Peace Prize winner Desmond Tutu. Fulfilling a pledge to serve just one term, he stepped down in 1999, remaining a global symbol of integrity until his death in 2013.

There are few more resilient figures in our recent history.

Enduring almost unimaginable suffering in prison, Mandela never lost hope that he would someday see his country freed of the yoke of apartheid. With the help of an international network of supporters, the pressure on the minority government in Pretoria finally became unbearable. In line with the tenor of the times that saw the Soviet bloc crumble, beginning in 1989, so did apartheid collapse shortly thereafter and Nelson Mandela was set free.

What prepared him to show such amazing resilience?

Mandela's father was a counselor to the king of the Thembu tribe, and after his father died, Mandela, at the age of twelve, became the king's ward and was influenced by tales of his ancestors' resistance to colonial rule. He wrote in *Conversations with Myself* (Farrar, Straus and Giroux, 2010): "After supper we would listen enthralled to my mother and sometimes my aunt telling us stories, legends, myths and fables which have come down from countless generations, and all of which tended to stimulate the imagination and contained some valuable moral lesson."

His identity and pride in his South African heritage were being formed and would inform the way he conducted his life.

He became a lawyer and political activist, and joined the African National Congress, then and now the biggest political party in the country.

One important aspect of a resilient character is the ability to use the past to put the present into perspective. It helps to bounce back if you realize your ancestors have faced the same issues or worse. Learning how they reacted back then can help you formulate a response now. For Mandela, his tribal ancestors gave him the strength to resist.

Always a vocal opponent of apartheid, the system begun in 1948 by South Africa's white-led minority government, which denied basic human rights to 90 percent of the country's people, Mandela finally saw it abolished with his election as president in 1994. But long before that, Mandela came to the attention of the white authorities as a troublemaker and was banned from politics in 1952 and declared a "restricted person."

After continuing his activism anyway, which led to several arrests, in 1961 he became the leader of an armed resistance group, called Spear of the Nation. In 1964, while still in prison for various offenses, he was tried with ten others for sabotage.

At the trial, he didn't mince words about the injustice of it all. He noted that he was escorted to the witness box by a white orderly, to face a white prosecutor before a white judge. How could the scales of justice be balanced in such a setting?

At the end, he gave what came to be known as his Speech from the Dock (witness box), which came to exemplify his philosophy. "During my lifetime I have fought against white domination, and I have fought against black domination. I have cherished the ideal of a democratic and free society in which all persons live together in harmony and with equal opportunities. It is an ideal which I hope to live for and to achieve, but if needs be, it is an ideal for which I am prepared to die."

Mandela and seven others were convicted of sabotage and sentenced to life in prison. He was held mostly in isolation on Robben Island, a prison known for its terrible conditions.

No South African should "wallow in the joy of freedom," he wrote, while many, including children, live in abject poverty.

There was no wallowing about Mandela. As soon as he was released from prison he began working toward freedom for all South Africans, not just himself. He believed that people were divided not by diversity, ethnicity, religion, or culture; the dividing line was rather between those who cherished democracy and those who did not.

He knew that the path to freedom involved more than "the right not to be oppressed"; it would be a long and difficult road that must include living in a way that "respects and enhances the freedom of others." It was a mindset that had to be changed and nurtured.

Resilience means never giving up. The fight isn't over until every victory is won.

Studying the deeds and words of Nelson Mandela reminds us that the human spirit can endure just about anything when there is still hope for freedom and justice. Few of us will be called on to suffer as he did. But we can all follow his example of fierceness in fighting for what's right, but of grace and reconciliation when the battle is won.

Lessons

Nelson Mandela's life after being released from twenty-seven years in jail is a lesson for us all.

- Don't get mad, get even. Good winners make victory all the more sweet.
- Never give up when your cause is just.
- Know that you have support—from friends, family, coworkers—even when times seem dire.
- Strength is character.
- Family stories with moral overtones are important to help build character for the next generation. This is your obligation.

Václav Havel

Vision is not enough. It must be combined with venture. It is not enough to stare up the steps, we must step up the steps.

—Václav Havel

Václav Havel was a Czech playwright, dissident, political prisoner, and, much to his own surprise, president of Czechoslovakia (as it then was) after the Velvet Revolution of 1989. His is a remarkable story of resilience.

The year 1989 was the most significant one in European history since 1945 and the end of World War II. A popular uprising led by shipyard electrician Lech Wałęsa, who like Havel became president of his country, toppled the Soviet-backed government in Poland. The same soon happened in Hungary, and the Berlin Wall came down in November. The next

month, Havel became president of Czechoslovakia and Ro-
manian dictator Nicolae Ceauşescu was felled and executed
on Christmas Day. The Soviet Union collapsed two years
later.

We may say that the entire turn of events in Eastern Europe
during this time was a display of the victory of resilience over
oppression.

Havel gave a speech before a joint session of the U.S. Congress in 1990, shortly after becoming president. He was greeted
by a thunderous standing ovation from the senators (including
Daniel Patrick Moynihan; see chapter 8) representatives, and
guests. The speech is so good, and so reflective of his character,
that I hope you will all watch it or read it. You can find it in the
C-SPAN archives at https://www.c-span.org/video/?10917-1/
czechoslovakian-president-address, if you're interested.

Havel, by then the Czech president, told Congress he had
been arrested just the year before and had no idea he'd wind up
as president. He had thought the proposal to make him president was a joke. After all, he would need to be nominated and
confirmed by the same legislature that had imprisoned him. But
it happened—unanimously.

Havel embodies the suddenness and unexpectedness of the
fall of the Soviet bloc in 1989, and his rapid rise from political
prisoner to president was not entirely unlike the latter transition
of Nelson Mandela in South Africa. As a dissident actor and
playwright he was known for the playfulness and almost impish
delivery of his speeches. He used humor rather than bombast to
make his points. The humor was often directed at himself: How
was it possible this humble playwright would become president
of his country? He's a humble playwright, not a lofty official.
And if he's dizzied by the speed of history, so must everyone
else be.

Self-deprecating humor is often a trait of the resilient. If you don't take yourself so seriously, your predicament may not seem as bad as it is. That can lead to hope.

But he could also discuss broader issues, and his advocacy of freedom of expression and thought was dead serious. These freedoms enable everything else. In the U.S. Bill of Rights, for example, there's a reason freedom of speech is in the First Amendment.

The ability to see the full picture from details is another worthy character trait. It's what the best teachers, and leaders, do instinctively. Havel credited his experience as a playwright, who needed to cram everything he wanted to say about human life into two hours, with giving him more experience than most politicians in trying to understand what was happening in the world. It also made him a gifted communicator, in his own way up there with Mandela, Moynihan, and Margaret Thatcher. Another gifted communicator, I would argue, is Volodymyr Zelenskyy, a former actor/comedian who was elected president of Ukraine in 2019. He became the fearless leader who has challenged and pleaded with other countries to help Ukraine resist the Russians, who invaded in February 2022. He generally appears in interviews—and even addressing the U.S. Congress—wearing an olive-green crew neck sweater, in solidarity with his countrypeople who are fighting for their land and freedom.

The unraveling of the Soviet bloc, literally happening as Havel spoke, opened for him the same possibilities that Giscard saw, ones we discussed in chapter 2. Havel also knew it would take work and U.S. aid, and he devoted a lot of his time to cultivating that support. He put it in terms of a democratic and free Eastern Europe being in the United States' best interests, which it surely was. He pointed out tirelessly that a free and democratic Czechoslovakia, as it then was, would be a bulwark against Russian expansion and would eventually fully participate in Europe.

He himself played a major role in realizing Giscard's prediction that Poland and Hungary would join NATO by 1999, as I mentioned in chapter 2. He often joked that he had never attended school for presidents, so he could act in that office only as his experiences directed him. Those experiences led him to recognize the power of freedom of action and expression, and that's what he promoted.

He knew that because of human nature, it might be impossible to form a true democracy or to enable all people to equally enjoy its fruits. But it's vital to try and to keep trying.

Soviet domination, he often said, taught him and his country resilience. He put great store in the human spirit. He didn't give in to despair but rather clung to hope. The ability to explain this difference is a key character trait. Tell the truth but identify solutions, not just problems. Though they differed politically, Havel and Thatcher agreed on this point. She once said admiringly of one of her ministers: "Everyone else brings me their problems. He brings me solutions."

When Havel ended his speech to Congress, he brought down the house by switching to English and quoting Thomas Jefferson. It is not just words that matter; it is also deeds.

Wow.

There were other inspirational leaders in Eastern Europe during the pivotal 1980s—Poland's Lech Wałęsa springs to mind—but Václav Havel brought a unique level of moral clarity and quiet eloquence, fueled by a steadfast character.

He changed his country and the world.

Lessons

Václav Havel, like Nelson Mandela, went from jail to the presidency of his country, although on a different path. The lessons:

- Be prepared for the unexpected. You're unlikely to be suddenly named president, but if that unexpected promotion or acceptance to your number one university choice comes through, be ready to accept and perform.

- Think beyond the immediate. There are generally bigger-picture implications of your actions.
- Don't take yourself seriously all the time. Self-deprecation can be a tool to express a resilient character.

Susan B. Anthony and Emmeline Pankhurst

I declare to you that woman must not depend upon the protection of man, but must be taught to protect herself, and there I take my stand.

—Susan B. Anthony

I would rather be a rebel than a slave.

—Emmeline Pankhurst

Today it may seem incredible to us that in the last part of the nineteenth century and first part of the twentieth, women in the United States and Britain had to fight so hard, sometimes against violent opposition and even landing in jail, in order to secure the right to vote. The battle was ultimately won in both places largely because of the courage and resilience of two controversial but brilliant leaders, Susan B. Anthony in the U.S. and Emmeline Pankhurst in the U.K.

Both women endured the hatred of some in the public and many in government, but both have emerged as heroes. Anthony is honored on the one-dollar coin and Pankhurst is memorialized by a statue outside the U.K. Parliament in London and more recently by a statue in Manchester, her birthplace.

Susan B. Anthony

Anthony in some ways led the way for Pankhurst, although the final victories in both countries came but two years apart—

British women over the age of thirty were given the right to vote in 1918, and the Nineteenth Amendment of the U.S. Constitution gave women that right in 1920. Pankhurst lived to see it; Anthony did not.

Susan B. Anthony was born in 1820 in Adams, Massachusetts, to a Quaker father and a mother whose family had fought in the American Revolution. Anthony often said her Quaker upbringing taught her that everyone was equal in God's eyes. She moved to upstate New York, where she met William Lloyd Garrison and Frederick Douglass and began giving passionate speeches in favor of abolishing slavery, which she did live to see in 1865. She also advocated for equal pay for equal work, a cause that continues to this day. But it is as a suffragette leader that she is best known.

In 1848, the first Women's Rights Convention was held in Seneca Falls, New York, effectively kicking off the suffrage movement. Anthony didn't attend, but her mother and sister did, and Susan met the event's organizer, Elizabeth Cady Stanton, three years later. Anthony and Stanton would lead the campaign for women's suffrage for the next fifty years, speaking at demonstrations and rallies all around the country.

The Nineteenth Amendment to the Constitution, passed by Congress on June 4, 1919, and ratified by the states on August 18, 1920, says simply:

"The right of citizens of the United States to vote shall not be denied or abridged by the United States or by any State on account of sex."

These twenty-eight words ended nearly a century of campaigning by Anthony and others, but many women felt it wasn't enough.

In 1921, Alice Paul and Crystal Eastman proposed an amendment to guarantee all rights to women. This first version of the Equal Rights Amendment didn't make it out of

Congress, and it was repeatedly rejected over the years, but a later version passed in 1972 closely echoes the Nineteenth Amendment. It reads: "Equality of rights under the law shall not be denied or abridged by the United States or any State on account of sex."

The ERA has been ratified by enough states, but some legislatures have rescinded earlier approvals, and some ratifications came after a 1979 deadline imposed by Congress. The courts are still trying to sort this all out.

Anthony was arrested for trying to vote in the 1872 presidential election and fined $100 (even bigger money in those days) but refused to pay, telling her supporters, "Resistance to tyranny is obedience to God."

In her speech she insisted she had committed no crime but was simply exercising her right as a citizen guaranteed in the Constitution. No state could deny that right, she argued.

She could have stopped there and had an unassailable argument. Notice that she used unemotional and irrefutable facts to set out her case. Understatement beats overstatement every time.

In referring to the Constitution, she said:

It was we, the people; not we, the white male citizens; nor yet we, the male citizens; but we, the whole people, who formed the Union. And we formed it, not to give the blessings of liberty, but to secure them; not to the half of ourselves and the half of our posterity, but to the whole people—women as well as men. And it is a downright mockery to talk to women of their enjoyment of the blessings of liberty while they are denied the use of the only means of securing them provided by this democratic-republican government—the ballot.

Again, these are facts that are impossible to refute. It sets up all the rest of her argument.

If a state makes gender a qualification for voting, or holding other rights, then the result is to disenfranchise half of the people. She equated such a government as not a democracy but an "odious" aristocracy.

The resulting oligarchy pits father, brothers, husband, and sons over mother, sisters, wife, and daughters in every home. Women become subjects, not equals.

She invoked famous men, such as Daniel Webster, to make the case for women's rights. It came down to the question, Are women people? There could be only one answer. Therefore, under the Constitution, no state has the right to abridge a person's rights.

From the twenty-first-century viewpoint it's hard to argue with this reasoning, but it took five decades until the vote was secured for women. Talk about resilience!

Anthony was a canny promoter of her ideas, in an age well before the internet or television. During the July 4, 1876, celebration of America's centennial in Philadelphia, which she was invited to attend but not at which to speak, she came onstage anyway and read out a Declaration of the Rights of Women of the United States, written by herself, Stanton, and Matilda Joslyn Gage on behalf of the National Woman Suffrage Association. It's an indelible document that rings true even today.

While the nation is buoyant with patriotism, and all hearts are attuned to praise, it is with sorrow we come to strike the one discordant note, on this one-hundredth anniversary of our country's birth. When subjects of kings, emperors, and czars, from the old world join in our national jubilee, shall the women of the republic refuse to lay their hands with benedictions on the nation's head?

She described poetically why women experienced injustice.

Our faith is firm and unwavering in the broad principles of human rights proclaimed in 1776, not only as abstract truths, but as the cornerstones of a republic. Yet we cannot forget, even in this glad hour, that while all men of every race, and clime, and condition, have been invested with the full rights of citizenship under our hospitable flag, all women still suffer the degradation of disfranchisement.

She presaged the feminist movement that would come one hundred years later by denying the "dogma of the centuries, incorporated in the codes of all nations—that woman was made for man—her best interests, in all cases, to be sacrificed to his will." No, women were not asking for special privileges; they were simply seeking equality.

Although the groundwork for the Nineteenth Amendment had been laid before Anthony's death in 1906, it didn't pass Congress until 1919 and went into effect the next year after ratification by the states.

There's little doubt it would not have passed even then without the resilience of Susan B. Anthony.

She was a perfect embodiment of intellect, morality, righteous indignation, and resilience. As we've seen and will see later, these traits don't often show up in people, but when they do, they can change the world.

Emmeline Pankhurst

Emmeline Pankhurst was born in Manchester, England, in 1858 and, following the example of her activist parents, became involved in the suffrage movement at age fourteen, joining the short-lived Women's Franchise League. She eventually joined the Independent Labour Party, led by Keir Hardie, and continued her agitation for suffrage. She also became an activist for the poor, often distributing food, and became in Manchester an elected official serving the homeless.

She later grew impatient with the Labour Party's inaction on women's suffrage and founded the Women's Social and Political Union (WSPU), which sought attention through violent protests, sometimes smashing windows or assaulting police. Pankhurst and her daughter, Christabel, were frequently jailed. "Deeds, not words, are our motto," she wrote. Emmeline Pankhurst was first arrested and jailed in 1908 when she tried to deliver a petition to Prime Minister Asquith. She would be arrested six more times before women got the vote.

The WSPU continued organizing, and in June 1908 drew a then-unheard-of crowd of five hundred thousand people to Hyde Park to demand the vote. A couple of WSPU members later threw rocks at 10 Downing Street. Various members of the WSPU went on hunger strikes to protest their arrests. After yet another suffrage bill fell short in Parliament in 1910, Pankhurst led three hundred women to march on the House of Commons, to be met by police led by then Home Secretary Winston Churchill (see chapter 6). More arrests followed. Pankhurst staged a hunger strike herself while in Holloway Prison in 1912 and was force-fed until she threatened to smash a clay jug over the head of a jailer.

With violent protests and even the occasional arson, the WSPU became the Women's Party, and ran Christabel Pankhurst for Parliament in 1917, the first election in which women were allowed to run, if not vote. She lost narrowly.

Emmeline Pankhurst never denounced violence as a means for women to bring attention to their cause, though she always tried to limit it to property damage, such as breaking the windows of men's clubs or tearing up men's-only golf club greens.

During World War I the WSPU halted its violent demonstrations and encouraged young men and women to aid the war effort. By the end of the war in 1918, the suffrage movement won the Representation of the People Act, which gave the right to vote to all men over the age of twenty-one and women over the age of thirty.

The first nation to grant women the right to vote was Norway, in 1913 (some colonies, provinces, and localities had granted this right previously), and many more followed during and just after World War I, including Canada (1917), the U.K. (1919), and the U.S. (1920). Women in France couldn't vote until 1944.

In the U.K., women got the vote in two stages: The 1918 Representation of the People Act granted the right to some women over the age of thirty; the 1928 Equal Franchise Act granted it to all women over the age of twenty-one.

As the suffrage movements in both the U.S. and Britain still struggled, Pankhurst visited the United States and gave this notable speech in Hartford, Connecticut, on November 13, 1913. I quote the gist of it, especially the biographical parts, but the entire speech is worth reading.

"I am here as a soldier who has temporarily left the field of battle in order to explain—it seems strange it should have to be explained—what civil war is like when civil war is waged by women," she said. Further, she stood before them as "a dangerous person, under sentence of penal servitude in a convict prison." She looked like neither a soldier nor a convict, yet she was both, she told them.

Her audience likely noticed the irony.

If her American audience had any doubt, here was a militant dedicated to her cause, fighting the same battle as American suffragettes. This was serious.

To help them understand why she was fighting, she told them that no one would be surprised if a man from Russia or China, for example, who was denied representative rights, would be justified in becoming a revolutionary to procure his due rights.

Why is it different for a woman? she challenged.

If she sounded frustrated, that's because she was. She was particularly vexed by newspaper reports of the U.K. struggle, which she felt were unfair.

Damage to property was not done to convert anyone to women's suffrage, she said. It was a political action by people shut out of politics by their lack of the right to vote.

The damage to property she described that day was breaking windows of shops and smart clubs in protest.

But the damage, she argued, was necessary and selective.

Sounding like many of her successors in the civil rights and anti-war movements of the 1960s, she added: "Well, in our civil war people have suffered, but you cannot make omelets without breaking eggs; you cannot have civil war without damage to something. The great thing is to see that no more damage is done than is absolutely necessary, that you do just as much as will arouse enough feeling to bring about peace, to bring about an honorable peace for the combatants, and that is what we have been doing."

She then detailed the escalation of the conflict and how women made the best of a horrible situation. Imprisoned and treated like criminals, women learned of the need for prison reform.

She called it a valuable experience, but ultimately it was unjust to send political agitators to prison for asking for justice.

Her words are a memorable rallying cry, perhaps also a warning.

"Women are very slow to rouse, but once they are aroused, once they are determined, nothing on earth and nothing in heaven will make women give way; it is impossible."

It's unclear exactly what effect her words had on her audience that day, but the U.S. suffragette movement did emerge victorious in 1919.

Pankhurst became solidly anti-Bolshevik after the 1917 Russian Revolution and ran as a Conservative Party candidate in the 1928 election, an effort cut short by her ill health. She died shortly before women over twenty-one were given the right to vote.

Lessons

Susan B. Anthony's and Emmeline Pankhurst's passionate advocacy of women's right to vote has lessons for us all.

- It can take a long time to change a society. Courage, patience, and resilience not only impress others but they also eventually lead to change.
- Suffragettes in both countries resisted the police and caused property damage to attract attention. Do you agree with these tactics if the cause is just?
- Leaders act, they don't just speak.
- Sometimes a leader will cement the support of one group—say, women—before trying to add another group's support—say, men. Such a tactic, if used properly, is additive, not divisive.

Stephen Hawking

However difficult life may seem, there is always something you can do and succeed at.

—Stephen Hawking

At the start of his book *A Brief History of Time* (Bantam, 1988), which sold more than nine million copies, Stephen Hawking retells one of my favorite jokes. During a lecture on astronomy, a scientist described how the earth orbits around the sun and how the sun, in turn, orbits around a vast collection of stars called our galaxy. When he finished, a little old lady got up and exclaimed that this was all rubbish and the world was really a flat plane supported on the back of a giant tortoise. The scientist, feeling smug, asked: "What's the tortoise standing on?" To which his questioner replied: "You're very clever, young man, but it's tortoises all the way down!"

Stephen Hawking spent his life, including thirty years as the Lucasian Professor of Mathematics at the University of Cambridge, a chair once occupied by Sir Isaac Newton, debunking the tortoise theory and trying to understand, and communicate, how the universe really worked.

In his book *The Universe in a Nutshell* (Bantam, 2001), he postulated that the human spirit, seeking creativity and discovery, would never stand still and instead would always be "the center of an expanding horizon of possibilities." I like that phrase; think about it and try to picture yourself in that center.

Hawking expanded on this idea in *The Grand Design*, written with Leonard Mlodinow (Bantam, 2010). Humans are ever curious, always seeking answers. Could anyone gaze at the vast heavens and countless stars and not ponder existential questions, such as, "How does the universe work? What is the nature of reality? Where did all of this come from? Did the universe need a creator?"

We might occasionally consider these profound puzzles, but Hawking spent more than thirty years worrying about them all the time. His very lifespan—he suffered from the degenerative nerve disease ALS (amyotrophic lateral sclerosis) for fifty-five years—is a study in resilience.

From Ptolemy to Copernicus to Newton to Einstein to Hawking, scientists have tried to understand and describe the universe through mathematical and mechanical models. Modern physicists developed quantum mechanics and other tools to get to the Standard Model, also called the Theory of Almost Everything, which describes actions between bodies large and small, as outlined in Einstein's theory of relativity and other theories, but doesn't account for gravity. Einstein tried but failed, and Stephen Hawking and others have proposed various, not-yet-successful ideas. These include quantum gravity, string theory, and brane theory, often involving the existence of multiple dimensions and multiple universes, all of which are beyond the scope of this book.

Stephen William Hawking, CH, CBE, FRS, FRSA (Companion of Honor, Commander of the British Empire, Fellow of the Royal Society, Fellow of the Royal Society for Arts, Manufacture and Commerce), to give him all his honors, was born in Oxford, England, in 1942. By the age of twenty-one, after getting a BA degree at Oxford and during graduate work at Cambridge, he was diagnosed with an early-onset, slow-progressing version of ALS, also known as Lou Gehrig's disease (see chapter 6), which left him paralyzed and eventually unable to speak without electronic assistance. He was a visiting professor at the California institute of Technology before returning to Cambridge, and his frequent visits to the U.S. and growing worldwide fame earned him the Presidential Medal of Freedom, awarded by President Barack Obama in 2009.

Physicists have long posited the existence in the universe of gigantic masses of matter so dense that they suck everything in the neighborhood into them and never let anything, including light, out. Their existence is required by Einstein's Theory of Relativity but he never fully accepted that they were real. They are called black holes, and many people besides Einstein scoffed at the idea until they were actually observed fairly recently. Hawking's contribution to research on black holes was to figure out how to relate quantum mechanics to these things, coming up with something called the Hawking radiation—perhaps his most famous scientific contribution—which explains how some light appears to escape from black holes. His work helped push along the Theory of Almost Everything (see box on page 72) but didn't quite get there.

He spent much of his professional life having arguments with colleagues about such topics as whether information can ever escape from a black hole, whether or not the universe started as an infinitesimal singularity rather than in a Big Bang, whether the universe actually has a beginning or an end, whether the Higgs boson would ever be found (he said it wouldn't be, but it was), and whether time travel was possible. Heady arguments! According to a 2014 article in *Scientific American* by Lee Billings, Hawking threw a party in Cambridge in 2009, "complete with balloons, hors d'oeuvres and iced Champagne," but didn't send out the invitations until the next day, to see if any time travelers would show up. None did.

Stephen Hawking's *A Brief History of Time* and the subsequent movie on which it is very lightly based stand in a long line of books and television shows that brought complicated scientific ideas to a broad audience. It was preceded by Carl Sagan's immensely popular book and TV series *Cosmos*, as well as James D. Watson's *Double Helix*, about the discovery of the structure of DNA, and followed by popular astronomy and astrophysics books and shows by Neil deGrasse Tyson and others. These books by Hawking and others have led countless young people to pursue studies and careers in science.

The thread that connects all of Hawking's work is curiosity. As we have seen with other leaders, he possessed the innovator's ability to harness failure to lead to success, and the resilience to withstand physical and intellectual setbacks. His career also manifests the courage not only to overcome the ravages of ALS and at one point having to communicate by moving a cheek muscle but also to try to answer what may be the biggest questions in the universe and keep trying even when shown to be wrong.

After the Higgs boson was found, contradicting his prediction, Hawking proposed that Peter Higgs be given the Nobel Prize, and Higgs received the prize in 2013. Hawking's research on black holes led to many arguments and lost and won bets, and his concession that one of his theories on this topic was his biggest blunder. But even that blunder turned out to be at least partly correct.

Stephen Hawking died in 2018 at the age of seventy-six, having far outlived all the doctors' predictions of his expected lifespan with ALS (he lived with it for sixty years) and courageously continued to seek answers.

Lessons

Hawking's extraordinary example of the mind overcoming near paralysis of the body to make world-changing discoveries holds valuable lessons.

- The brain is the source of character. Physical disabilities can be overcome with a strong enough will.
- Communication is essential to innovation. Discoveries need to be widely known and understood. The form of communication matters little—it can be a tinny mechanized voice—as long as the content is compelling.

- Curiosity is everything. Even if you don't throw a party and invite everyone after it's over to see if time travel exists, try lots of things that you wonder about.
- There are no stupid questions, just stupid answers.
- If you ever think life has dealt you a bad hand, think of Stephen Hawking in his wheelchair, twitching his face muscle to communicate. Do you have the resilience to face your problems?

Chapter Five

BREAKING BARRIERS

Character cannot be developed in ease and quiet. Only through experience of trial and suffering can the soul be strengthened, vision cleared, ambition inspired, and success achieved.

—Helen Keller

As long as there have been societies, there have been barriers erected, intentionally or not, within those societies that prevent the equal access to success. Over the millennia, societies have been dominated by a particular sex, or religion, or race, or class, or tribe, or political alignment.

Again, we think of Dr. Martin Luther King Jr.'s quote about the centrality of character rather than one of these artificial distinctions. It takes a special person to defy conventional wisdom, or repressive authoritarianism, or entrenched thinking, to stand up for themselves and for everyone else in their society.

We'll look at barrier breakers who refused to be held down because of their sex, color, or political beliefs. Margaret Chase Smith was the first woman to serve in both the House and Senate, and the first to represent the state of Maine in either capacity. Bill Russell was the best basketball player of his generation and the owner of eleven NBA championship rings. But as one of the earliest Black players in college and in the NBA, he had to overcome racism and discrimination at every stage, emerging through the strength of his character as a role model for all. Julia Child was a prominent chef specializing in French cuisine at a time when most chefs were men. She was also among the first of many to bring cooking to television.

By breaking these barriers, they became role models for millions, but recognition wasn't their motivation. Rather, they were motivated by the same sense of justice that motivated Dr. King, believing that universal values need to be applied universally, and that by doing so, everybody benefits.

Margaret Chase Smith

> Standing for right when it is unpopular is a true test of moral character.
>
> —Margaret Chase Smith

Margaret Chase Smith of Maine was the first woman to be elected to both the U.S. House and Senate, a notable barrier to have broken, but is probably best remembered today for her early, courageous, and principled stance against her fellow Republican Joseph McCarthy and his Red-baiting in the 1940s and 1950s.

I'd like to offer Smith's character not just as an example of barrier breaking but also for courage, integrity, and transparency. There aren't many of her type around today in either party; we certainly could use a lot more.

Margaret Chase was born in Skowhegan, Maine, in 1897.

As was relatively common then, Smith succeeded her late husband, Clyde, as a U.S. representative, but then won reelection four times before winning the Senate seat in 1948. She was awarded the Presidential Medal of Freedom in 1989 by President George H. W. Bush.

Although she was the first woman to win election to both the House and the Senate, Smith wasn't the first woman to serve in either body. Rebecca Felton of Georgia was appointed to a Senate seat in 1922, twenty-six years before Chase was elected. There have been fifty-eight women appointed or elected to the Senate, with twenty-four serving as of 2022. Since Jeannette Rankin of Montana was elected in 1916, before women were allowed to vote (see chapter 4), 352 women have served in the House, plus 7 non-voting delegates, as of 2022. Nancy Pelosi was the first and only female Speaker of the House, and Kamala Harris the first and only vice president (and president of the Senate).

Smith's most famous speech was her "Declaration of Conscience" in the Senate on June 1, 1950, at the height of McCarthyism. It is extraordinary both for the courage it took to deliver it then, and for the lessons it offers us now. Chase had initially given some credence to McCarthy's charges that the State Department was infiltrated by Communists, asking him to provide her documents. When she saw that McCarthy actually had no evidence, even though she knew it might hurt her chances of being picked as Dwight Eisenhower's running mate in 1952 (she was among the first women to be considered seriously for this post) if she alienated McCarthy, who controlled Wisconsin's votes at the Republican Convention, she decided to speak out. McCarthy sat two rows behind her as she rose.

The speech contains many echoes to our character deficiencies today. As Mark Twain allegedly said: "History doesn't repeat itself, but it often rhymes." See if you can spot the rhymes below.

Her opening lines could well have been said yesterday, not seventy-five years ago.

I would like to speak briefly and simply about a serious national condition. It is a national feeling of fear and frustration that could result in national suicide and the end of everything that we Americans hold dear. It is a condition that comes from the lack of effective leadership in either the legislative branch or the executive branch of our government.

Remember, this was a Republican speaking in 1950, not today!

She said the Senate had devolved from the world's greatest deliberative body into a forum for invective and character assassination.

Sounds familiar?

She implored senators to search their souls, and their consciences, and uphold and defend the Constitution.

She was speaking, incredibly bravely, of the baseless accusations of Senator Joseph McCarthy that many government officials were Communists, which led to decades of Red-baiting and ruined lives. In this, she was at the time a lone voice in politics.

Today we might see history rhyming with this speech. There seem to be elements on both sides of the political spectrum who want to divide rather than unite. We could use more Margaret Chase Smiths.

Along with six other Republican senators, Smith prepared the "Declaration of Conscience."

It was a brave act, but although they were Republicans, they were Americans first. (A good reminder today for any elected official.) She criticized what she considered ineffective leadership of the Democratic administration as well as some Republican Party members who selfishly exploited "fear, bigotry, ignorance, and intolerance" for the sake of winning elections.

"It is high time that we all stopped being tools and victims of totalitarian techniques—techniques that, if continued here unchecked, will surely end what we have come to cherish as the American way of life," the declaration stated.

There was little reaction in the Senate Chamber to this

speech. McCarthy said nothing and quietly left. But he began a smear campaign against Smith and the co-signers of her declaration, derisively calling them "Snow White and the six dwarves."

We could surely use such a declaration of conscience today. With her speech and this declaration, Smith broke barriers well beyond those she had broken in getting elected. It is the best example of character to stand up for what you believe no matter the consequences, and with no regard for whether it is your "place" to do so. Margaret Chase Smith was an unlikely candidate to stand up to Joseph McCarthy, but it is to her credit that she did. Sometimes the improbable can be the most powerful.

Smith survived the smears and in 1954 had the pleasure of voting for McCarthy's censure, which effectively ended his career.

Despite the anti-McCarthy speech, which won her national attention, Smith was a generally conservative senator who favored increased defense spending from her perch on the Armed Services Committee, and enthusiastically backed the Vietnam War and the draft. These stances arguably cost her reelection in 1972, when she lost to Democrat William Hathaway.

Smith retired to Maine to establish her library and died in 1995.

Lessons

Margaret Chase Smith's life offers lessons of courage and integrity as well as breaking barriers.

- Speaking your mind may not always be popular but it will win you respect.
- A broken barrier is no guarantee of success or necessarily an indication of strong character. Actions must follow.
- Bullies rarely stand up to being called out.
- Whether Twain actually said it or not, history really does rhyme. Seeing parallels to past events is a useful tool for understanding today.

Bill Russell

> The idea is not to block every shot. The idea is to make
> your opponent believe you might block every shot.
> —Bill Russell

Bill Russell was a champion basketball player, a championship basketball coach, and a moral force for civil rights and justice until his death in 2022. It wasn't just his accomplishments, or his six-foot-ten-inch, 220-pound frame that garnered him respect. It was the force of his character. Bill Russell competed hard but was never dirty. He didn't break or even bend the rules and had little time for those who did. He didn't need trash talk to intimidate opponents. As a coach, he exuded quiet authority.

Above all, he seemed to be having fun, nowadays a relatively rare emotion among highly paid professional athletes. "To me, the most important part of winning is joy," he once said. "You can win without joy, but winning without joy is like eating in a four-star restaurant when you're not hungry. Joy is a current of energy in your body, like chlorophyll or sunlight, that fills you up and makes you naturally want to do your best."

This is also a measure of leadership and character. The best leaders enjoy what they're doing and transmit that feeling to their followers or employees. They may even smile or pump their fists upon occasion.

Character is almost always manifested in a strong moral base and sense of right and wrong.

A few years before his death, Russell saw ex-NBA star Charles Barkley complaining on a TV show about paying too much in taxes. Russell called Barkley:

"Yes, Mr. Russell?"

"Charles, be happy you're making a lot of money and they can tax you a lot. But there was a time when you were poor, when the cops came to your neighborhood, when you went to public schools, somebody else was paying those taxes, too."

"Yes, Mr. Russell." Barkley never complained about paying taxes again.

Bill Russell won two NCAA Championships, eleven NBA titles with the Boston Celtics, including two as player-coach; helped the U.S. win the 1956 Olympic basketball gold medal; and was the NBA's first Black coach. (Phil Jackson has eleven rings as a coach, with the Bulls and Lakers. Michael Jordan won six championships with the Bulls.) Russell won five Most Valuable Player awards. He was inducted into the Naismith Memorial Basketball Hall of Fame in 1975 as a player and in 2021 as a coach. (The only others inducted twice are Bill Sharman, Lenny Wilkens, Tom Heinsohn, and John Wooden. See page 119.) The trophy given to the NBA Finals Most Valuable Player was named in his honor in 2009. President Barack Obama awarded him the Presidential Medal of Freedom in 2011. He is the only basketball player to be awarded the country's highest civilian honor; the citation details his civil rights work.

William Felton Russell was born in Louisiana but grew up in Oakland, where his father was a janitor in a paper factory and eventually worked in a shipyard. Upon his mother's death, Bill Russell became withdrawn and would spend hours reading in the public library. During high school he ran track and began playing basketball, though he was still growing. He got one offer of a college scholarship, the University of San Francisco. He later wrote that USF was "a small school no one could find" and he "was a tall guy nobody wanted." Still it was a chance to go to college, which was what he really wanted.

Russell, along with future Celtics teammate and NBA Hall of Famer K. C. Jones, led USF to NCAA Championships in 1955 and 1956. He was the second player chosen in the 1956 draft and played or coached for Boston for the next thirteen years.

Among his teammates were Bill Sharman and Bob Cousy, maybe the greatest backcourt duo ever. I ran into Cousy some years ago at a Holy Cross college game and he told me that while he had the greatest respect for Sharman, "it was Russell who made the whole thing run."

During Russell's era, Black players, who had not been allowed into the league until 1950, three years after Jackie Robinson broke the color line in baseball, redefined the game.

Russell encountered explicit racism throughout his career and was active in the 1960s Civil Rights movement. In his autobiography, *Go Up for Glory* (Penguin, second edition, 2020), Russell recalled that frequently being called the N-word by white people pushed him on during basketball games. His house in a white suburb was defaced with excrement and racist graffiti. He and his black Celtic teammates were once denied service at a restaurant in Indiana after having been given the keys to the city by the mayor at an exhibition game. The men went to the mayor's house and tossed the meaningless keys at his feet.

Russell, as with most aspects of his life, kept his activism private—but pointed. At a meeting with Dr. Martin Luther King Jr. in Atlanta before the March on Washington and King's "I Have a Dream" speech in 1963, King invited Russell to join the dignitaries on the platform at the march. But Russell felt he'd be too much of a distraction and chose to sit in the second row of the audience instead.

He summed up his philosophy in his book as fighting for what he believed was right, without fear of consequences.

Russell embodied this ideal on the court and off. He later reflected on his success and what it took to get there. "I hope I epitomize the American dream. For I came against long odds, from the ghetto to the very top of my profession. I was not immediately good at basketball. It did not come easy. It came as the result of a lot of hard work and self-sacrifice. The rewards, were they worth it? One thousand times over."

There is plenty to unpack here in terms of character. What is the American dream if not a collection of character lessons? Remember, we're not going to generalize, and the American dream is an aspiration that's available to anyone: life, liberty, and the pursuit of happiness. Success is built on hard work and self-sacrifice. Facing down and overcoming barriers and long odds.

Elsewhere, Russell once said his proudest possession as a kid was his Oakland Public Library card. Learning is a classic way to overcome barriers, by equipping yourself with knowledge that nobody can take away. While Russell had far more formal education than, say, the largely self-taught Abraham Lincoln, the men shared a lifelong love of learning.

From the time he threw the key to the city back at an embarrassed mayor through his Hall of Fame induction and later advocacy work, Bill Russell exemplified effort, integrity, and grace, even when it wasn't easy.

In doing so, Bill Russell broke every barrier he faced.

Lessons

Bill Russell taught lessons every day on and off the court.

- Grace, integrity, and hard work can overcome any barrier.
- While athletics has long offered the opportunity for the underprivileged to advance in society, the relatively few who have done so have needed the strength, determination, and confidence to overcome barriers, vital character traits.
- Life is more than any profession, including professional sports. To be the best among thousands of talented engineers, athletes, or scholars requires a force of will we often see as character.

Julia Child

> Drama is very important in life. You have to come on with
> a bang. You never want to go out with a whimper.
> Everything can have drama if it's done right. Even a
> pancake.
>
> —Julia Child

Julia Child may have been the unlikeliest TV star ever. A
trained but amateur cook, she exuded enthusiasm with an in-
fectious laugh and a blowsy style, whether she was frying an
egg or deglazing the sediments in a pan for a complicated
sauce. She burned things, dropped stuff, and sometimes left out
an ingredient, all unflappably. The barrier she broke was making cooking fun and accessible to her vast TV audience. She
also broke what seemed to be barriers in many U.S. house-
holds to well-prepared, wholesome, and delicious food. Of her
PBS show *The French Chef*, she said, "I am neither one nor the
other," but to millions she was both.

In the introduction to the fortieth-anniversary edition of her
two-volume cooking bible, *Mastering the Art of French Cooking*
(Knopf, 1961, 2001), written with Louisette Bertholle and Simone Beck, Child explained that the first step in learning to
cook was learning how to eat! Surprisingly simple, right? But
her point was that if you didn't know how a dish was supposed
to taste, then how could you create it? Step two: You "learn
about great food by finding the best there is, whether simple or
luxurious. Then you savor it, analyze it, and discuss it with your
companions, and you compare it with other experiences."

Bear in mind that Child grew up in a middle-class Southern
California home, where the roast was overcooked to a bland
gray. It wasn't until she moved to Paris with her diplomat husband, Paul Child, and the Cordon Bleu cooking classes that followed, that her palate developed at the age of thirty-nine. ". . . up
until then, I just ate," she said.

And how did she get on in France, reportedly (and wrongly) generally thought of as the home of rude waiters and aloof people? Just fine. She found the French to be sweet, generous, polite, and gentle, contrary to the stereotype.

Ignore stereotypes, which can be harmful, and approach all with a positive attitude.

Julia had it figured out. "Just speak very loudly and quickly, and state your position with utter conviction, as the French do, and you'll have a marvelous time!"

When she began her PBS show, the biggest barrier she had to break wasn't being a woman on television (there were many others) but rather the barrier of postwar bland American cooking. Convenient boxed mixes, with all their unnatural ingredients, were popular.

When *The French Chef* debuted on WGBH in 1963, it was pretty much alone as a cooking show that demonstrated on-air recipes and cooking techniques of a single cuisine. Today there are dozens of such shows as well as dedicated food networks that showcase virtually every type of food imaginable. Julia Child, who died in 2004, would have been amazed at the success of *The Great British Baking Show*, *Iron Chef*, or any of Gordon Ramsey's high-volume efforts. Throughout the nine seasons of *The French Chef*, Julia was seemingly alone in her kitchen, competing against only herself, demonstrating the intricacies of boeuf bourguignon or pâté en croûte. She also hosted a number of other shows, including *Dinner at Julia's* and *Baking with Julia*.

She believed that too much fussiness and pressure in the kitchen discouraged a lot of would-be cooks and were barriers to better eating.

Julia was down-to-earth. Once she told her viewers not to

worry if they are alone in the kitchen and happen to drop the lamb. "You can always just pick it up. Who's going to know?"

Everyone makes mistakes. A secret to cooking is to learn how to correct a mistake, if possible, or just move on.

Her relaxed attitude gave home cooks permission to have fun in the kitchen.

Julia was confident enough in her own skin also to make fun of herself when warranted. During a show on making crème brûlée, essentially custard with a sugar crust burnt using a small blowtorch, she looked up, pointed the flame at the audience, and said: "I think every woman should have a blowtorch."

She was a firm believer that you could rarely go wrong in the kitchen with good ingredients and a good attitude, no fancy masterpieces required. In that regard, she was ahead of her time. Fresh, quality ingredients—that's the essence of today's farm-to-table movement.

For Julia Child, the kitchen was her artist's studio, a place to use imagination. She wanted everyone to share both the creative opportunities and love of cooking.

She was no stranger to butter, cream, and fat. Why fat? Because fat gives flavor. But what about the health craze that started in the U.S. at roughly the same time as her PBS show? Her characteristic playfulness made clear her view of the no-fat trend in the 1970s. "The only time to eat diet food is while you're waiting for the steak to cook."

She did not fret about her legacy. She said sooner or later the public will forget you. What remains important, however, is the individuals you have influenced, many times unknowingly. Above all—friendship; tend and nurture it.

Lessons

Julia Child offered cooking lessons, but also life lessons.

- Nobody can prevent you from breaking a barrier except yourself. Whether it's running a marathon or cooking a four-course gourmet meal, it won't happen unless you train for it and then try it.

- Jump in. Child knew nobody and spoke little French when she arrived in Paris with her husband. She left a Francophone who could cook, and with friends who helped her write her books and create her TV shows.
- Fail, burn a few vol-au-vents before figuring it out.
- Don't take yourself too seriously; have fun in what you're doing.

Chapter Six

COURAGE

It is curious that physical courage should be so common in the world and moral courage so rare.

—Mark Twain

Mark Twain's distinction between physical and moral courage is worth keeping in mind as you read this chapter. We're going to look at three men and two women. Two of them, Arthur Ashe and Lou Gehrig, exhibited physical courage, but all are remarkable for their moral courage. Both Gehrig and Ashe, after their playing days ended, fought dread diseases and raised awareness to help other sufferers. Winston Churchill and Edith Cavell became, in different ways, embodiments of the struggles of a nation at war.

Courage is bravery, but it's also a character trait built from self-knowledge and empathy. To be courageous, you need to be fully aware of the situation and forge ahead, because your course of action will benefit others. Bravery without these elements can easily veer off into foolishness.

Many of the people profiled in other chapters of this book routinely displayed courage as a character trait, as well as the other traits we'll examine. John McCain, Jimmy Stewart, Nelson Mandela, and Václav Havel spring to mind. There are everyday examples of courage in the news, of firefighters skillfully navigating a burning building to save trapped residents, or police capturing armed suspects.

But courage doesn't always require a physical act of bravery. In your own lives, do you have the courage to stand up to a bully harassing a friend? Do you have the courage to admit your mistakes? Do you have the courage to try something that's out of your comfort zone?

The stories of Churchill, Ashe, Gehrig, Florence Nightingale, and Cavell will give you tools to act courageously and recognize courage in others. We know instinctively that courageous people are people of character, but we rarely stop to try to understand why that is so. I'll give it try.

Winston Churchill

> You can measure a man's character by the choices he makes under pressure.
>
> —Winston Churchill

Over many years I've read and admired a lot of what Winston Churchill has written and what others have written about him. He is a larger-than-life figure commemorated by a larger-than-life statue just off Parliament Square in London inscribed with just one word: Churchill. A memorial plaque in Westminster Abbey reads: Remember Winston Churchill.

He is impossible to forget, a British bulldog of a war leader and prime minister, a giver of inspirational speeches that live on, and a writer of histories that won him a Nobel Prize in Literature, somewhat to his chagrin.

Winston Leonard Spencer Churchill was born at Blenheim Palace, his family's ancestral home in Oxfordshire, England, in 1874. (It's a magnificent house and the grounds are now open to the public and worth a visit.) Churchill studied at Sandhurst, the British equivalent of West Point, and joined the army as a second lieutenant in 1895. He served with great courage and in many cases wrote articles for various newspapers about battles in Cuba, India, and Sudan.

He left the army in 1898 and later covered the Boer War in South Africa as a journalist and briefly rejoined the army to fight in it. He was elected to Parliament as a Conservative in 1900 at his second try, the youngest member ever at age twenty-five. Switching parties, Churchill got his first government post under Liberal prime minister Henry Campbell-Bannerman in 1906 as a junior colonial office minister. He was later president of the Board of Trade, overseeing labor and business matters, and home secretary, a post that brought him into direct conflict with the women's suffrage movement (see chapter 4).

Churchill was the government minister in charge of the navy when World War I broke out in 1914. After some war setbacks, notably the disastrous Battle of Gallipoli, Churchill was forced out as first lord of the Admiralty. He quit the government, though he remained an MP.

Note that if Churchill had given up after the setbacks, the trajectory of history likely would be quite different. But as we have seen, as with so many others with character, he did not give up.

War setbacks then or political setbacks later would not deter him from his duty that lay ahead.

He went to fight on the western front in Belgium in 1916 and rejoined the government the following year.

When the war ended in 1918, Churchill was given the task of demobilizing, or reintegrating, soldiers back into normal life. He returned to the Conservatives in 1924 and was named chancellor of the exchequer, equivalent to our treasury secretary, a post he held until the Tories lost the 1929 election, stock markets crashed, and the Great Depression took hold.

Early on, Churchill recognized and spoke out about two threats to Europe's future: the Communist regime in the Soviet Union and Hitler's rising influence in Germany. He strongly opposed appeasing Mussolini in Italy and Hitler in Germany.

When Britain declared war on Germany in September 1939,

Churchill again became first lord of the admiralty under Prime Minister Neville Chamberlain.

Just off Horse Guards Road near St. James's Park in London is a discreet door into a discreet government building, once known as the New Public Offices building, leading to a warren of underground rooms from which the British government essentially operated during much of World War II. Formally the Cabinet War Rooms, but more popularly the Churchill War Rooms, scholars and tourists can now see where the prime minister, his cabinet, and his top military officers met to plan strategy. The rooms are small and claustrophobic, and with some staff spending twenty-four hours a day inside during the war, there were even sun lamps provided to give them a little vitamin D. The whole museum is fascinating. I went there for the first time intending to spend an hour and stayed all day. There's now a Churchill Museum within the War Rooms complex featuring many Churchill artifacts.

Churchill gave dozens of memorable speeches, but I'm going to briefly quote just two of his most powerful, and let them display his courage, eloquence, and leadership.

On May 10, 1940, with Britain at war with Germany, Winston Churchill became prime minister, succeeding Neville Chamberlain. When Churchill met his cabinet on May 13 he told them, "I have nothing to offer but blood, toil, tears, and sweat."

He repeated that phrase later in the day when he asked the House of Commons for a vote of confidence in his new all-party government.

". . . blood, toil, tears, and sweat." This, of course, became a rallying cry for the British and illustrates the power of courage to move an audience and, indeed, an entire nation. Note the color and specificity of the language. Blood, toil, tears, and sweat remained an indelible image of what the British went through during and after the war.

This was about as honest a statement as possible on the suffering that lay ahead. It was another statement born of courage: I'm not going to sugarcoat this. Buckle up.

His stirring speech, near poetry, lives on as one of the famous in recent history.

We shall fight on the beaches, we shall fight on the landing grounds, we shall fight in the fields and in the streets, we shall fight in the hills; we shall never surrender, and even if, which I do not for a moment believe, this Island or a large part of it were subjugated and starving, then our Empire beyond the seas, armed and guarded by the British Fleet, would carry on the struggle, until, in God's good time, the New World, with all its power and might, steps forth to the rescue and the liberation of the old.

We shall fight on the beaches . . . became perhaps the second-most quoted line from this remarkable speech. How better to rally a nation for what lay ahead?

Two weeks later, Churchill was back in the House of Commons, to deliver another indelible call in which he predicted, ". . . if the British Commonwealth and Empire lasts for a thousand years, men will still say, 'This was their finest hour.'"

In August, the nightly bombing raids and air battles that came to be known as the Battle of Britain raged. The country needed his bravery and determination as beacons in a dark time.

Throughout the war, often working and sleeping in the underground War Rooms to escape the German bombardments of London, Churchill continued to inspire by example, taking care to be visible and not seen as cowering.

After months of pleading, Churchill persuaded U.S. president Franklin Roosevelt to provide Britain crucial supplies and arms under the 1941 Lend-Lease Act. It was a crucial point in the war, helping Britain survive until the Americans entered the war after Pearl Harbor in December 1941. Throughout the war, Churchill and Roosevelt maintained the closest of relations.

Though Churchill led an ultimately successful war effort, and was probably the only British leader who could have done so, the Conservatives lost the postwar 1945 election largely on domestic issues. Churchill remained a vigorous leader of the opposition and, with his eyes on the postwar divisions of Europe, gave one of his most famous speeches in 1946 while visiting Westminster College in Fulton, Missouri, standing next to President Harry Truman.

He warned of the "Soviet sphere," famously describing it as an "Iron Curtain" that "descended across the continent." The phrase "Iron Curtain" became a symbol, an image that the public could understand.

This speech marked the beginning of the Cold War, which didn't really end until the dissolution of the Soviet bloc began in 1989 (see chapter 4).

Winston Churchill won a Nobel Prize, but not for anything to do with his government service. He was awarded the Nobel Prize for Literature in 1953, according to the committee, for his "mastery of historical and biographical description as well as for brilliant oratory in defending exalted human values." By that time Churchill had delivered his "Blood, Sweat, and Tears" speech and many others like it during World War II, and had written *The World Crisis*, a history of World War I, and the six-volume *Second World War*, the final volume of which appeared in 1953, probably too late to have been considered. He wrote *A History of the English-Speaking Peoples* after he received the Nobel Prize. Most of his works are still in print. Churchill reportedly received news of the prize gleefully until he learned it was for literature, not the Peace Prize he had badly wanted and never received.

Churchill became prime minister again in 1951, remaining in office until 1955. He was in poor health throughout this second term but managed to focus on rebuilding Britain's depleted housing stock and maintaining the Special Relationship with the United States (see chapter 8), making many visits. In retirement, he continued speaking, writing, and painting until his death in 1965.

Lessons

Winston Churchill's lessons are indelible. Courage. Inspiration. Doggedness.

- Leaders inspire by displaying courage, both in word and deed.
- Courage gives leaders the resiliency to bounce back after defeat.
- People know when leaders are being honest with them, especially when they can see the truth themselves.

Arthur Ashe

> True heroism is remarkably sober, very undramatic. It is not the urge to surpass all others at whatever cost, but the urge to serve others at whatever cost.
>
> —Arthur Ashe

This quotation is quintessential Arthur Ashe, embodying his modesty, self-control, selflessness, and above all his courage. While he won three Grand Slam singles championships and led the U.S. to the Davis Cup three times, being the first Black athlete to do so, he also courageously fought prolonged battles against racism, at home and in apartheid South Africa, and against heart disease and AIDS. He was one of the rare intellectuals in tennis.

Arthur Ashe was the first Black tennis player to win an NCAA singles title (for UCLA in 1965) and was also the winner of the first U.S. Open Championship in 1968, the Australian Open in 1970, and Wimbledon in 1975. Even though many men and women have won far more major championships, Ashe is a tennis legend, and the world's biggest tennis arena, Arthur Ashe Stadium at the Billie Jean King National Tennis Center in New York, was built and named in his honor in 1997, just four years after his death.

Why this acclaim? Because of his character. Ashe personified dignity, patience, calmness, fair play, and above all immense courage in the face of racism and two major illnesses. I recall being at a meeting about the stadium with Mayor Rudy Giuliani and others. When it came time to suggest names, someone offered the name of Bill Tilden, a great champion of a much earlier era. Someone else suggested Arthur Ashe, and that was that. Nobody ever suggested naming a stadium after Jimmy Connors or John McEnroe, two great but volatile players.

Arthur Ashe, a direct descendant of slaves, began playing tennis at age seven on the Blacks-only tennis courts in Richmond, Virginia, where his father was a caretaker. Throughout his childhood and young adulthood, Ashe experienced discrimination. (His story somewhat mirrors those of Venus and Serena Williams, many years later.)

In 1961, while attending high school in St. Louis under the sponsorship of a renowned Black tennis coach, Ashe needed special permission to participate in a previously whites-only scholastic tennis tournament, which he helped win for his school. While he may have been seething, he never used racism as an excuse for his difficulties. "Racism is not an excuse to not do the best you can," he said.

Ashe went to UCLA on a tennis scholarship, joined the ROTC, and later served two years in the Army, leaving as a second lieutenant. During these years he was the first African American selected for the U.S. Davis Cup team, helping his country win the cup three times, and won both the U.S. Amateur Championship and the U.S. Open in the same year (1968), the first and only man to have done that.

He did all this as the first or only Black in most of these tournaments, exhibiting an unshakable calmness and confidence. There were no outbursts, no drama. His coaches told him early on never to argue a line call if the ball was within two inches in or out. He never did.

This attitude was a major character trait of Ashe's. No matter how you may feel inside, try to project control and confidence. It can provide a mental edge and maybe lead to victory.

To elaborate, self-confidence is a key to success. And the key to self-confidence? Preparation, he said.

The year 1968 also saw the assassinations of Dr. Martin Luther King Jr. and Robert Kennedy. Ashe had been reluctant to speak out about the discrimination he faced until that pivotal year of 1968, but then he started giving political speeches and joined Jackie Robinson and other athletes in supporting a ban on South Africa's participation in the Olympics because of apartheid. Ashe fought apartheid the rest of his life. After several years of denials, because of apartheid, he finally gained entry in 1973 to the South African Open, after telling organizers he wouldn't play before a segregated crowd. Apartheid was finally abolished with the release from prison of Nelson Mandela, toward the end of Ashe's life (see chapter 4).

In 1975, on his ninth try, Ashe beat Jimmy Connors to win Wimbledon, again the first Black to do so. This victory meant a lot to him.

"As an African American athlete, I have experienced racism as a tennis player, going way back," Ashe once said. "I have played extraordinary matches under unbelievable circumstances, but Wimbledon tied my whole life together."

In 1979, Ashe suffered a heart attack and underwent a successful quadruple-bypass operation. He needed another open-heart surgery in 1988, and he and his family believe he was likely infected with the HIV virus during that surgery. He was diagnosed as HIV positive in 1988 but didn't publicly disclose this until 1992, when he founded the Arthur Ashe Foundation for the Defeat of AIDS. He died from AIDS-related pneumonia in 1993.

> AIDS (acquired immunodeficiency syndrome) ravaged the world in the 1980s, until prevention measures and medications reduced the toll. More than one hundred thousand Americans died of AIDS between 1981 and 1991, more than thirty thousand in 1990 alone. While the HIV virus that causes AIDS can be transmitted through sexual contact, contaminated blood transfusions like the one received by Ashe killed far too many before transfusion protocols were tightened.

We can learn from Ashe's view on life. "I have always tried to be true to myself, to pick those battles I felt were important," he said. "My ultimate responsibility is to myself. I could never be anything else."

Lessons

Arthur Ashe displayed lessons of courage with every backhand and every action of his various foundations.

- You don't need to shout to make your voice heard.
- Courage comes from strong grounding in what is right and wrong.
- Rather than complain, fight against adversity.
- Always be true to yourself; that is your responsibility.
- Arguing may get you attention, but moving on without arguing gets you a stadium named after you.

Lou Gehrig

Yet today I am the luckiest man on the face of the earth.
—Lou Gehrig

The name Lou Gehrig today conjures up images of a Hall of Fame baseball player known for his fielding, hitting, and ability to play every day—the Iron Horse—for seventeen years. But it also brings to mind a man, crippled by ALS, the disease that would also come to bear his name, saying goodbye at Yankee Stadium in 1939.

Both Gehrig's baseball career and his brave fight against ALS were products of a courageous, resilient, and determined character, evident early on in his life.

Gehrig was born in New York City in 1903, the son of German immigrants, his father a sheet-metal worker, his mother a maid. Childhood was difficult. His three siblings all died young, and his father was often drunk, so Lou became the family's support. He spoke German until he also learned English at age six. In 1920, he showed his baseball talent early, leading his High School of Commerce team to a victory over Lane Tech High School by hitting a grand slam home run out of what is now Wrigley Field in Chicago.

He went to Columbia University on a football scholarship but switched to baseball as a pitcher, and left after two years to join the Yankees' minor league affiliate in Hartford. He played sporadically for the big-league team in 1923 and 1924, until the fateful day in 1925 when Yankees first baseman–slugger Wally Pipp had a headache. Gehrig replaced him and never gave the job back.

In Gehrig's era, of course, baseball players and athletes in general earned much less than they do today. It's estimated

Gehrig earned about $360,000 in his entire career, worth about $7 million today. Not bad, but nothing compared with the nine-figure contracts of today's superstars. Babe Ruth's salary reached $80,000 a year in 1930 (about $1.5 million in today's dollars), higher than that of then president Herbert Hoover. When asked to justify this, the Babe answered: "I had a better year."

Gehrig had perhaps his best season in 1927, on arguably the best team in MLB history. He hit .373 with 47 home runs and 175 RBIs, as the Yankees won 110 regular season games and swept the Pittsburgh Pirates in four games to win the World Series. Though Gehrig won the league MVP, most baseball aficionados remember 1927 as the year Babe Ruth hit 60 home runs.

After a decade of stardom and unprecedented success for the Yankees, Gehrig, not yet diagnosed with ALS, found himself weakening and unable to run or hit reliably. He broke his consecutive game streak on May 2, 1939, and never played again. He was diagnosed with ALS at the Mayo Clinic in June.

Lou Gehrig was called the Iron Horse, for good reason. Once he replaced the Yankees first baseman Wally Pipp, who had a headache, on June 2, 1925. June 2 is now celebrated in every MLB park as Lou Gehrig Day, to raise money for ALS research. (There's a great trivia answer for you.) Gehrig went on to play 2,130 consecutive games, a record broken by Cal Ripken Jr. (2,632 games) in 1995. (Another trivia answer.) Nobody has come close to Ripken—or Gehrig, for that matter—and it's unlikely anyone ever will. Over his career, Gehrig had a batting average of .310, 2,721 hits, 493 home runs, and 1,995 runs batted in. He was an All-Star seven times in a row (1933–39), was the American League Most Valuable Player in 1927 and 1936, won the Triple Crown (highest batting average, most home runs, most runs batted in) in 1934, and won six World Series championships with the Yankees. He was inducted into the National Baseball Hall of Fame in 1939, a few months after his retirement, an exception to the rule that players had to wait five years after retirement before being on the ballot. Gehrig had a plaque on a pedestal near the fence in center field of old Yankee Stadium (alongside manager Miller Huggins and Babe Ruth) that was finally moved to the stadium's Monument Park in 1973. For Hollywood's take on his courage, check out *Pride of the Yankees*, a 1942 Sam Goldwyn movie with Gary Cooper as Gehrig and Babe Ruth and Bill Dickey, among others, as themselves.

His farewell speech, delivered to more than sixty thousand fans packed into Yankee Stadium on July 4, 1939, Lou Gehrig Appreciation Day, just a few weeks after his illness forced him to retire, is remarkable and worth looking up.

He said that, despite the bad break he'd gotten with his health, he was the luckiest man on the face of the earth.

What an amazing statement. Lucky despite a horrible affliction. There's no self-pity, only gratitude for the fans' affection.

He praised the officials and teammates who were present, including Yankees owner Jacob Ruppert, umpire Ed Barrow, Miller Huggins, and manager Joe McCarthy. It takes a special person of character to shout out to teammates when the day is all about you. This is genuine, not faked, humility.

He found kind words for the old rival, the Giants, who gave him a fruit bowl and two candlesticks. Sportswriter John Kieran, at the behest of the Yankees team, wrote a poem that was inscribed on a trophy along with all the team members' names and cherished by Gehrig in his final years.

During the ceremony, held between games of a double-header between the Yankees and the Washington Senators, New York mayor Fiorello La Guardia called Gehrig "the perfect prototype of the best sportsmanship and citizenship."

Legendary manager Joe McCarthy added that it was a sad day for everyone when Gehrig announced he was leaving baseball. He did so because he felt he was a "hindrance to the team," McCarthy said. "My God, man, you were never that."

Gehrig, barely able to stand, finished his speech: "So I close in saying that I might have been given a bad break, but I've got an awful lot to live for. Thank you."

Imagine the physical and moral courage it took to stand before all those people and deliver that speech.

He'd live for another two years, racked by the progressive nerve degeneration of ALS. He died at home in the Bronx on June 2, 1941, by coincidence sixteen years to the day he had replaced Wally Pipp on first base.

Amyotrophic lateral sclerosis (ALS), also known as motor neuron disease or Lou Gehrig's disease, is a rare degenerative disease that causes sufferers to progressively lose control of their limbs and other bodily functions. There is no known cure. ALS can work quickly—Gehrig died two years after being diagnosed—or slowly—Stephen Hawking survived fifty-five years with the disease, which gradually got worse. Research toward finding better treatments and a cure continues, supported by the Ice Bucket Challenge and other initiatives.

Lessons

Lou Gehrig taught lessons with his baseball bat on the field and his courage in the face of his devastating illness.

- Life isn't fair. It takes courage to count your blessings despite bad breaks.
- Humility in the face of success will inspire others to admire and follow you.
- Courage is sometimes knowing when to stop.

Florence Nightingale and Edith Cavell

I attribute my success to this—I never gave or took any excuse.

—Florence Nightingale

I can't stop while there are lives to be saved.

—Edith Cavell

Two heroic British nurses, operating in peril in two different wars, changed modern health care and embodied courage as a character trait. Florence Nightingale, giving up a comfortable life to tend British troops in the Crimean War, famously walking the wards at night, became known as the "Lady with the Lamp." Edith Cavell, a nurse working on the western front in Belgium, treated German, Belgian, and British wounded alike, and for her efforts in smuggling out soldiers to the Netherlands she was executed in 1915 for treason by the Germans.

Britain's Princess Anne, the Princess Royal, commemorated the one hundredth anniversary of Cavell's execution with a speech in Brussels in 2015. The princess, then the president of the organization Save the Children, nicely summed up the two nurses' contributions and their lasting importance:

"Both Nightingale and Cavell were too modest, in reality they were pioneers. Both bravely tackled prejudice and suspicion to establish nursing as a respected profession, after all it was neither reputable nor a profession before they started. Both overcame low expectations about what women could and should achieve and took physical risks with their own lives."

Florence Nightingale

I am of certain convinced that the greatest heroes are those who do their duty in the daily grind of domestic affairs whilst the world whirls as a maddening dreidel.
                                    —Florence Nightingale

Florence Nightingale was born in 1820 in Florence, Italy, to wealthy British parents. She entered nursing in 1844 but was by then also an accomplished statistician and chronicler of journeys, including trips to Greece and Egypt.

In 1854, her friend Sidney Herbert, then the U.K. secretary at war, sent Nightingale and thirty-eight nurse-volunteers to help rehabilitate a notoriously unhealthy hospital at Scutari, now called Üsküdar, in Istanbul, some three hundred miles from where British troops were fighting in Crimea. They were an early forerunner of Doctors Without Borders, though with government backing.

Nightingale believed, and often said: "The very first requirement in a hospital is that it should do the sick no harm." That wasn't true at Scutari, where patients were dying by the dozens.

She was so troubled by the unsanitary conditions and rampant infections at the hospital that Nightingale posted on the social media of the day (a letter to the *Times* of London), asking the government to do something. They responded by commissioning the famous architect of bridges and other structures, Isambard Kingdom Brunel, to design a prefabricated hospital that could be shipped to the war zone. The Renkioi Hospital was up and running by 1856 and was said to have cut the death rate at Scutari by 90 percent.

One of the basic reforms Nightingale instituted wherever she worked was simple hand washing, the forerunner of today's routine scrubbing and gloving. Back then the need wasn't so obvious; Pasteur hadn't yet developed his theory of germs. She advocated washing hands frequently, and faces, too.

She also believed in opening the window to allow fresh air to flow into hospital rooms. "To attempt to keep a ward warm at the expense of making the sick repeatedly breathe their own hot, humid, putrescine atmosphere is a certain way to delay recovery or to destroy life," she said.

This was all part of Nightingale's then-revolutionary idea that nursing should be thought of as a skilled profession within the medical field, rather than as an afterthought.

Though she considered nursing an art, she didn't particularly like the word *nursing*, with its overtones of mothering. Instead the profession—and she did raise it to a profession—ought to encompass the many requirements to return a patient to health, if possible, such as cleanliness, fresh air, and a proper diet.

She also bristled at the condescension most doctors had for nurses back then. To Nightingale, doctors and surgeons were all well and good, but it was the nurse who gave patients back their dignity and their lives. "It is often thought that medicine is the curative process. It is no such thing; medicine is the surgery of functions . . . nature alone cures." What nursing does is "to put the patient in the best condition for nature to act upon him."

That's a big responsibility.

Nightingale's fame was fanned by loving characterizations in British newspapers of the time. A *Times* correspondent, who called her a "ministering angel," wrote: "When all the medical officers have retired for the night, and silence and darkness have settled down upon these miles of prostrate sick, she may be observed alone, with a little lamp in her hand, making her solitary rounds."

Note that Nightingale had no public relations staff, but with stories like this she didn't need one. Even Henry Wadsworth Longfellow got into the act, with a poem in the November 1857 issue of the *Atlantic Monthly*, titled "Santa Filomena," which raised her to a legend.

You can read the full poem if you wish, but this gives you an idea of the image he made indelible:

> *On England's annals, through the long*
> *Hereafter of her speech and song,*
> *That light its rays shall cast*
> *From portals of the past.*
> *A lady with a lamp shall stand*
> *In the great history of the land,*
> *A noble type of good,*
> *Heroic womanhood.*

Countless newspaper illustrations, often fanciful, showing a nurse carrying a lamp followed, as well as the 1929 London play *The Lady with the Lamp* (starring Dame Edith Evans as Nightingale) and a film of the same title in 1951. The Church of England commemorates her life every year on August 10, the day of her death in 1910. She was the first woman awarded the British Order of Merit, in 1907.

After Crimea, Nightingale spent the next forty years trying to improve nurse training and public health. Using money raised after she returned from the war, she set up the Nightingale Home and Training School for Nurses at St. Thomas' Hospital in London. Her 1859 *Notes on Nursing* was used in many nursing schools and to train home nurses and cemented her reputation as the founder of modern nursing.

Building on her early proficiency with statistics, she pioneered graphic presentations of results, and is credited with inventing the polar-area diagram, a fancy kind of pie chart. She used them for reports on everything from medical care in Crimea to the Indian sanitation system.

Lytton Strachey, in his 1918 *Eminent Victorians,* pricks the bubble a bit by painting Nightingale not so much as a saint but rather a driven woman rebelling against the strictures of Victorian England, and one whose obsessions drove her to embrace mysticism near the end of her life. He shows her as a caring nurse but also a tough-as-nails perfectionist administrator often berating her colleagues and staff and always berating the government in London, which wasn't doing enough to help.

Fair enough. But her courage, foresight, and accomplishments certainly justified her fame, if not her deification. Hospital sanitation was changed forever, and nurses gained a worthy model to emulate.

Next time you're in London, check out her statue, which stands on a high plinth in Waterloo Place, just off Pall Mall.

Edith Cavell

> Patriotism is not enough. I must have no hatred or bitterness for anyone.
>
> —Edith Cavell

Those words, spoken just before her execution, grace the base of the statue of Edith Cavell in Trafalgar Square in London, alongside the inscriptions: For King and Country, Faithful until Death, Humanity, Devotion, Fortitude, and Sacrifice.

This was her life in a nutshell, a life propelled by courage.

Edith Cavell was born in Norfolk, England, in 1865, became a nurse at the age of thirty, and in 1907 took charge of a nursing hospital, the Berkendael Medical Institute in Brussels. After World War I broke out in 1914, she tended to casualties of soldiers from both sides. During the occupation of Belgium by the Germans, she helped organize a resistance cell that moved British, French, and Belgian soldiers to the then-neutral Netherlands. Cavell was arrested by the Germans in 1915, charged with treason, and executed that year.

World War I (1914–1918) was the deadliest conflict in history (until it was topped by World War II) and marked the end of the old order in Europe, resulting in the changing of national boundaries, many of which were redrawn after WWII and in some cases are still being contested today. It was the first conflict in which aircraft and dynamite were available to inflict heavy losses. The devastation of the war caused the worsening of the 1918–1920 flu pandemic, during which millions more died.

Unlike most of the others profiled in this book, Cavell gave no famous speeches and didn't win the Nobel Prize, so we'll use mainly her actions as a measure of her character.

Cavell trained and began her nursing career in London, after a stint looking after her ailing father. After she was recruited to head the Berkendael Institute in Brussels, she became instrumental in training Belgian nurses, using techniques and methods pioneered by Florence Nightingale and raising the level of care substantially. Her nursing work in Belgium alone should have been enough to make her famous.

As World War I broke out, Cavell's clinic was taken over by the Red Cross. It treated any German wounded who turned up, as well as British and French fighters and civilians, in keeping with the quote on her statue: "I must have no hatred or bitterness for anyone." This fact would later be used as a plea for mercy for her by German diplomats, to no avail.

By the standards of the time, this was extraordinary. The

Geneva Conventions that govern the treatment of enemy combatants weren't adopted until 1929 and modified in 1949. Even
today in some places enemy soldiers aren't routinely given care.

In November 1914, as the Germans occupied Belgium, she
began smuggling wounded British and French soldiers and
civilians to the Netherlands, aided by members of a resistance
group, one of whom betrayed her to the German authorities.

During her ten-week imprisonment, she admitted that she
had sheltered in her house and then helped to escape about
two hundred men. Since some of these men went on from the
Netherlands to Britain, with which Germany was at war, she
was convicted of treason.

As Princess Anne noted in her speech commemorating a
century since Cavell's death, when the priest at the execution
said, "We will remember you as a heroine and as a martyr," she
replied, "Don't think of me like that; think of me as a nurse
who tried to do her duty."

Nonetheless, Cavell's execution was widely reported in British and American newspapers, and became a rallying cry, and
propaganda tool, for the war effort. She was the most famous
British woman to die in the war. Anti-German posters in the
U.K. showed her grave. She was instantly portrayed in movies, including the 1916 Australian film *The Martyrdom of Nurse Cavell*,
the 1918 U.K. film *The Woman the Germans Shot*, and an American film, *The Cavell Case* the following year.

The centennial of her death was marked by numerous paintings and musical compositions, as well as a commemorative
five-pound coin.

Her legacy has been lasting. The Cavell Nurses' Trust, established soon after her execution, continues to provide scholarship and aid for nursing students more than a century later. The
Anglican Church, which doesn't canonize saints in the Catholic
fashion, recognizes her in its Calendar of Saints on October 12,
the date of her execution. Even before the Trafalgar Square
statue, erected in 1920, Canada named Mount Edith Cavell in

the Canadian Rockies in 1916. She has been commemorated with a street and hospital in Brussels and even Cavell Corona, a geological feature on Venus.

Cavell left a final letter to her nurses on the eve of her execution. It reads in part:

> When better days come our work will again grow and resume all its power for doing good. . . . a good heart will sustain you in the hard moments of life and in the face of death. I may have been strict, but I have loved you more than you can know.

Lessons

Florence Nightingale and Edith Cavell revolutionized nursing, under fire, and in Cavell's case at the expense of her life. Both offer lessons.

- Courage can come from anywhere.
- Heroism often arises from simple humanity.
- Professionalism—in nursing, for example—can save lives.
- Believe in the value of what you are doing, even if it may go against the norms and perceptions of the times. Often this is how progress is achieved.

Chapter Seven

LOYALTY

Character is higher than intellect. A great soul will be strong to live as well as think.

—Ralph Waldo Emerson

Loyalty is not just your dog sticking to your side during a walk or licking your hand at home (though both are nice when they happen). To display loyalty to a cause or a friend is a visible character trait that inspires loyalty in return, trust, and respect in others. It's one of the hardest character traits to develop, since it involves others, but it is one of the most worthwhile.

It may be loyalty to your husband (who may happen to be president) and later loyalty to heartfelt causes, such as human rights for all. Or it may be loyalty to the team you lead, coaching them up and never down, and always teaching, because losing can be as instructive as winning. Or it could be the loyalty to his country and fellow soldiers that leads a horribly treated prisoner of war to refuse to go home until other prisoners who got there before him were released.

Think of the people who have inspired your loyalty and those who are loyal to you. Which character traits do you admire in people and which do they admire in you? If you're having trouble answering this question, this chapter might help.

Eleanor Roosevelt

> Only a man's character is the real criterion of worth.
> —Eleanor Roosevelt

Eleanor Roosevelt was the most prominent American woman in the mid-twentieth century, a loyal supporter of her husband's policies as president—she was the longest-serving First Lady—but was known mostly for her fidelity and outspokenness on the most difficult problems facing the U.S. and the world, especially those of the dispossessed and displaced after World War II.

She was appointed the first U.S. delegate to the United Nations General Assembly in 1946, a post she held until 1953. In 1948, as chairwoman of the Human Rights Commission, she was instrumental in drafting the Universal Declaration of Human Rights. She later chaired President John F. Kennedy's Presidential Commission on the Status of Women. Harry Truman called her "the First Lady of the World."

Anna Eleanor Roosevelt was born in 1884 to a prominent family and was the niece of Theodore Roosevelt and a distant cousin of her husband, Franklin Delano Roosevelt. Like many daughters of wealthy families back then, she was educated at a private finishing school, hers in London, where among other things she became fluent in French. She married Franklin in 1905 in New York, with President Teddy Roosevelt giving the bride away, as her parents had passed away.

Roosevelt bore six children and nursed her husband through the illness that left him paralyzed beginning in 1921. She remained loyal despite Franklin's infidelities. Eleanor was active in politics, assisting her husband's successful campaigns for New York governor in 1928 and president in 1932.

She redefined the role of First Lady, which under her immediate predecessors had largely involved ceremonial activities at the White House. She held regular press conferences, to which only female reporters were invited, in contrast to her husband's all-male meetings. She was the first First Lady to speak at a Democratic National Convention, where in 1940 her husband was nominated for a third term. She wrote a daily newspaper column and hosted a weekly radio show.

She used her position to correct injustices, when possible. In 1939, Marian Anderson, the famous contralto who had performed in major concert halls in the U.S. and Europe, was scheduled to sing at Constitution Hall in Washington, D.C., but the Daughters of the American Revolution (DAR) canceled the event. Why? The Philadelphia-born Anderson was Black.

Keep in mind, just three years earlier Eleanor Roosevelt had invited Marian Anderson to sing at the White House; they had become friends.

Roosevelt saw the injustice of the DAR rejection for what it was and, with others such as the NAACP and Interior Department Director Harold Ickes, arranged for the concert to be held instead in front of the Lincoln Memorial. On Easter Sunday 1939, an integrated crowd of seventy-five thousand heard Marian Anderson's voice rise from the steps of the memorial. It was a historic moment for civil rights.

During World War II, Eleanor lobbied with limited success for increased U.S. acceptance of refugees from Europe. She made frequent visits to U.S. troops during the fighting.

After Franklin died in 1945, Eleanor remained a popular public figure, known for her championing of human rights for everyone, regardless of race or country, and largely through the then-nascent United Nations.

The United Nations was founded in San Francisco in 1945 and headquartered in New York City and Geneva, Switzerland. It comprises 193 members, who sit in the General Assembly, but major decisions on peace and security are made by the 15-member Security Council. The U.S., China, Russia, U.K., and France (the winning side in World War II) are permanent members with veto power over any Security Council action; the other 10 members rotate among the general membership. While often criticized for inefficiency and powerlessness, the UN provides peacekeeping services in many ongoing conflicts, and its agencies such as the World Health Organization play a vital role in fighting pandemics and the spread of many diseases.

As a U.S. delegate to the UN in 1946, Eleanor Roosevelt was instrumental in drafting the Universal Declaration of Human Rights in 1948. It reads in part:

> *Whereas recognition of the inherent dignity and of the equal and inalienable rights of all members of the human family is the foundation of freedom, justice and peace in the world,*
>
> *Whereas disregard and contempt for human rights have resulted in barbarous acts which have outraged the conscience of mankind, and the advent of a world in which human beings shall enjoy freedom of speech and belief and freedom from fear and want has been proclaimed as the highest aspiration of the common people,*
>
> *Whereas it is essential, if man is not to be compelled to have recourse, as a last resort, to rebellion against tyranny and oppression, that human rights should be protected by the rule of law,*
>
> *[. . .]*
>
> *Now, therefore*
>
> *The General Assembly*
>
> *Proclaims this Universal Declaration of Human Rights as a common standard of achievement for all peoples and all nations.*

Its thirty articles cover everything from slavery to non-discrimination to torture to equal protection under the law to free elementary education to forced marriage. Sadly, it has never been effectively applied in many countries, even today.

Eleanor Roosevelt delivered her most famous speech, "The Struggle for Human Rights," in Paris in September 1948 as the

UN was considering the Universal Declaration of Human Rights she had worked so hard on. I'm going to paraphrase a few passages not only because they display the resoluteness of her character but also because we once again see history rhyming.

Bear in mind that this was just after World War II had devastated Europe, including the capital in which she was speaking.

She started by defining human rights as those of freedom of speech and the press, freedom of religion and worship, freedom of assembly and the right of petition (in the First Amendment to the U.S. Constitution), and the right to be secure in one's home and free from unreasonable search and seizure and from arbitrary arrest and punishment.

While we may take these ideas for granted today, they weren't back then, especially as what Churchill had called the Iron Curtain descended across Eastern Europe (see chapter 6).

She warned that authoritarians and dictators often twisted those concepts to their own perverted views of freedom, but these ideas had nothing to do with dictatorships nor oppression.

She was denouncing the propaganda of the Soviet Union, which continues in Russia through different guises today. We also see variations of this perverse commandeering of the words of freedom all over the world—as they do sometimes in our own politics. It should be remembered that George Orwell wrote his novel *1984* in 1948 (yes, he just reversed the last two digits) and his Big Brother character was a great believer in disinformation. Freedom is freedom.

Roosevelt felt passionately that the denial of these basic freedoms in totalitarian societies of those times, including the Soviet Union, was the greatest problem facing the world. She likened the struggle to those of the French Revolution and the American Revolution.

A patriot in the true sense, Roosevelt then presented American values as the respect for the rights of others and the ability to make our own laws, and pointed out that the freedoms of speech, press, information, and peaceable assembly are the tools Americans use to create their way of life.

She rejected any sort of authoritarianism, some of which is still being preached today.

She then turned to the centrality of free, fair elections, in which the loser accepts the results. Anybody hear the rhyming?

She was also, despite many epithets hurled at her by enemies at the time, a firm capitalist, saying that capitalism with some regulatory restraints had created great prosperity for a lot of people.

But there's still work to be done.

Roosevelt wouldn't live to see most of the gains of the civil rights movement, but she sensed they would come.

She was for expanding human rights around the world, perfecting capitalism, rejecting propaganda, and assuring freedom everywhere.

It's hard to find any of these sentiments controversial, but they were back then and still are in some quarters of our politics.

Eleanor Roosevelt is one of the relatively rare historical figures who embody character. (Mandela, Churchill, and Mother Teresa are others.) Her traits of moral clarity, compassion, and honesty shine through all of her speeches and works.

Lessons

Eleanor Roosevelt started from a high perch as First Lady and became one of the most famous women in U.S. history. Her lessons:

- Pick a cause and stick with it.
- If you have a platform, use its influence for all it's worth.
- Leadership emerges when times are hardest.
- Starting in a privileged position is great, but it's what you do from there that counts.
- Define bedrock values—such as freedom of speech and the press, free and fair elections, civil and human rights— and remind the public of their importance in a democracy.

John Wooden

> Be more concerned with your character than your reputation, because your character is what you really are, while your reputation is merely what others think you are.
>
> — John Wooden

John Wooden coached such basketball royalty as Bill Walton and Kareem Abdul-Jabbar while winning a record ten NCAA championships and earning himself the nickname Wizard of Westwood, for the neighborhood which is home to the University of California at Los Angeles. (Wooden hated the nickname. He didn't want to be thought of as a wizard—some sort of magician who does things on the sly.)

Wooden inspired such loyalty in his players that he usually had the pick of the best high school prospects and molded them into great players and great teammates. He always thought of himself as a teacher, a role in which loyalty is essential.

I met him in person only once, while he was on a recruiting trip to my high school, St. Charles, in Columbus, many years ago. We won the game against our rivals—the number one team in the state—and after the game Coach Wooden came to our dressing room under the stands and sat next to me on the bench.

Everybody was really excited and shocked that he was there. I got all puffed up. He looked at me in a long-measured way and I'll never forget what he said.

"Son," Wooden said, "you're not big enough to play on the inside and you're not fast enough to play on the outside. I recommend you go to college." He was right. And I did, but not to play basketball.

It was this insight that made him such a successful recruiter for UCLA. In his book *Becoming Kareem: Growing Up On and Off the Court* (Little, Brown, 2017) Kareem Abdul-Jabbar, then Lew Alcindor, recalls that during his recruiting visit to UCLA in 1965, Wooden looked him in the eyes, complimented him on his high school grades, and said: "For most students, basketball is temporary. But knowledge is forever. You can only play basketball for so long, then you've got to get on with the rest of your life." Alcindor, who was recruited by pretty much every college team in the country, was sold.

The relationship between John Wooden and Kareem Abdul-Jabbar endured for forty-five years, from the recruiting visit in 1965 until Wooden's death in 2010 at age ninety-nine. Abdul-Jabbar wrote about this in *Coach Wooden and Me* (Grand Central, 2017), saying the man with whom he won three NCAA Championships was more than a basketball master, he was a role model.

Wooden said it all came down to teaching; more than the games or the tournaments, he loved team practices. For him, teaching during practices, he said, was what coaching was all about.

His lessons went beyond the skills of basketball.

"I had three rules for my players," he said. "No profanity. Don't criticize a teammate. Never be late."

John Wooden obeyed these rules, and a lot more, himself. I kept in touch with him as time went on and told him I went to Notre Dame. Here I was a sophomore in college and he's a four-star coach and he took my calls. On one of those calls, he told me to take care of the little people. By that he meant the people who would never be in the headlines or play center for UCLA but would live their lives with integrity. They are the soul and character of the U.S., he told me.

Before his coaching career, John Wooden was a star player himself at Purdue, being named to the All-America team in the 1930, 1931, and 1932 seasons. He became the head coach at UCLA in 1948, staying twenty-seven years. During that time, his teams had the longest winning streak ever, eighty-eight games between 1971 and 1974, and thirty-eight consecutive NCAA tournament wins. He was the first of five men inducted into basketball Hall of Fame as both player and coach. (The others are Bill Sharman, Lenny Wilkens, Tom Heinsohn, and Bill Russell; see page 83.)

Coach Wooden is also known for inspirational books and speaking.

In the book *Coach Wooden's Pyramid of Success*, coauthored with Jay Carty (Revell, 2005), Wooden showcased a diagram of various character traits arranged in triangles to make a pyramid. The base comprises Industriousness, Friendship, Loyalty, Co-operation, and Enthusiasm. These traits support Self-Control, Alertness, Initiative, and Intentness. Those in turn support Condition, Skill, and Team Spirit, the basis for Poise and Confidence, with it all topped by Competitive Greatness.

Let's look at a few of these traits and how they fit into Wooden's career and character. Wooden, correctly, thought letting players be responsible for their own actions was the best way to inspire loyalty.

While Wooden was the clear leader of his teams, he needed all of his players to be leaders for the team to succeed.

Intentness: John Wooden loved cerebral players like Bill Walton and Kareem Abdul-Jabbar. They always played with intention, not just physical force. When two teams are evenly matched, thought often makes the difference.

Team Spirit: His players always knew what was expected—to give their best at all times.

Confidence: Wooden never minded confidence, though not cockiness, in players whose on- and off-field performance merited it.

Competitive Greatness: Again, a key to Wooden's character. It's what made his teams great for so long, year after year. He instilled the character that made talented players want to succeed again and again. And be good people.

Lessons

John Wooden's loyalty to his players as human beings as well as athletes, and his loyalty to basketball, offer valuable lessons.

- Loyalty comes from trust. Trust comes from honesty.
- Try to inspire the loyalty that John Wooden did in Kareem Abdul-Jabbar, loyalty that endured for fifty years.
- Teamwork is a pure example of loyalty to one's teammates and oneself.
- Talent is wasted without leadership.

John McCain

It is your character, and your character alone, that will make your life happy or unhappy.

—John McCain

John McCain, war hero, prisoner of war, U.S. senator, candidate for president, and self-defined political maverick, seemed to embody the independent character of the American West. But his character was also shaped by the military lineage from which he descended, especially from his father and grandfather, both of whom served in the Navy before him.

McCain is perhaps best known for three things. The first was his courageous behavior as a prisoner of the North Vietnamese, refusing early release offered because his father was the admiral in charge of U.S. forces. McCain said he'd stay until all men captured before him were released, and he continued to endure lack of medical care for his arms broken in the plane crash, torture, and solitary confinement. The second was his gracious concession after losing the 2008 presidential election. The third was his dramatic and decisive thumbs-down no vote on a Republican motion to repeal the Affordable Care Act, known as Obamacare, in 2017, cementing his maverick reputation.

The first showed loyalty to his comrades. The second showed loyalty to his country's ideals. And the third showed loyalty to his ideals.

"Glory is not a conceit," he once said. "It is not a decoration for valor. Glory belongs to the act of being constant to something greater than yourself, to a cause, to your principles, to the people on whom you rely and who rely on you in return."

John Sidney McCain III was born in 1936, and, following family tradition, graduated from the U.S. Naval Academy at Annapolis and was commissioned as a fighter pilot. He was shot down over North Vietnam in 1967 and remained a prisoner in the Hoa Lò Prison, known as the Hanoi Hilton, for five years.

Being in captivity made him fall in love with his own country, and not just for the comforts that he was lacking as a prisoner.

"I loved it for its decency, for its faith in the wisdom, justice, and goodness of its people. I loved it because it was not just a place, but an idea, a cause worth fighting for," he said. "I was never the same again; I wasn't my own man anymore; I was my country's."

John McCain's home for more than five years as a prisoner of war was Hoa Lò Prison, better known as the Hanoi Hilton. The original name means "stove" or "furnace." It was built by the French to house prisoners during the colonial era, and then called Maison Centrale, and by the North Vietnamese for prisoners of war during the Vietnam War. The first U.S. soldier was imprisoned there in 1964. Vietnam continued to use the prison after the war, for political prisoners.

It was demolished in the 1990s but there's still a museum on the site, which any local guide will gladly take American tourists to see.

After his release and recovery, John McCain commanded a flight-training squadron in Florida and became the Navy's liaison to the U.S. Senate in 1977. Though he never said so publicly, he likely thought he could do a better job as senator than some of the people he liaised with. He was elected to the House in 1982 and to the Senate in 1986. He ran unsuccessfully for president in 2008, losing to Barack Obama. His controversial choice of Alaska governor Sarah Palin as his running mate probably didn't help, nor did the 2007–2008 financial crisis that began during the administration of fellow Republican George W. Bush.

McCain's politics were conservative, pretty much in line with those of Ronald Reagan and Barry Goldwater, the Arizona senator whose seat McCain would eventually occupy. In 1983, McCain opposed the creation of the federal holiday to honor Dr. Martin Luther King Jr., but later said he was wrong to do so.

He once nicely summed up his philosophy: What endures in life is the honor earned and love given when sacrifice is made for something greater than self-interest.

He also said, in an echo of western U.S. self-reliant thinking: "I don't believe in destiny. We are not born to become one thing or another, left to follow helplessly a course that was charted for us by some unseen hand, a mysterious alignment of the stars that pulls us in a certain direction, bestowing happiness on some and misfortune on others." This way of thinking is liberating—you are not limited by anything preordained.

McCain's imprisonment in Hanoi was one of the hardest mental and physical tests imaginable. While he did make one statement at the behest of his jailers, for which he later said he was ashamed, the beatings continued after he refused to make any more. When he was finally released, along with one hundred or so other prisoners, in 1973, he couldn't raise his arms above his head, and required years of physical therapy.

As I mentioned above, one of the best showcases of McCain's character was when he lost the 2008 election to Barack Obama. During the campaign McCain publicly corrected a questioner who said she didn't trust Obama "because he's an Arab." McCain told her she was wrong and that Obama was "a fine man."

Soon after the results were clear on election night, McCain addressed his followers in one of the most gracious concession speeches I've ever heard. He said he admired and commended Obama for "inspiring the hopes of so many millions of Americans" who had once thought they had little influence in the election of a president.

Despite their political differences, his admiration for Obama was sincere. He thought Obama's election was historic, and history was important to McCain. He invoked Theodore Roosevelt's invitation of Booker T. Washington to dine at the White House—a watershed moment in the struggle for civil rights—and he regarded the free and fair election of an African American as president as another step in the right direction, affirming the fairness of Americans. Significantly, he had no trouble accepting the verdict of the electorate, though it must have been personally disappointing.

As I write this in early 2024, there is still a GOP faction that refuses to accept the results of the 2020 election. How refreshing to recall the words of this GOP candidate promising to help the Democrat who beat him. After all, to McCain, country came first.

What a remarkable testament to both patriotism and the moral compass of John McCain. President Obama also referred to finding a purpose greater than oneself in his first inaugural address.

One of McCain's most consequential votes as a senator was

on a Republican bill that would have gutted Obama's principal achievement as president, the Affordable Care Act, which reformed the health insurance market. McCain stoutly opposed Obamacare but felt the Senate bill didn't adequately protect Social Security and Medicare, a key issue for Arizona's aging population. Against the wishes of President Donald Trump and Senate Majority Leader Mitch McConnell, McCain stood before the Senate clerk well after midnight, and turned his thumbs down on the GOP bill.

Above all, McCain was a patriot, loyal to his country and its ideals. "Despite our differences, much more unites us than divides us. We are fellow Americans, an association that means more to me than any other. . . . Being true to our conscience, being honest with ourselves, will determine the character of our relations with others. That is a concise definition of integrity."

Lessons

John McCain embodied loyalty to his fellow prisoners and his country, lessons we all need.

- Be magnanimous in victory and gracious in defeat.
- Loyalty to yourself and colleagues is the foremost test of character.
- Your loyalty will often overshadow the exact details of your actions or votes or statements at any time.

Chapter Eight

INTEGRITY

Fame is a vapor, popularity is an accident, riches take wings, those who cheer today may curse tomorrow and only one thing endures—character.

—Harry Truman

When we say somebody has integrity, we mean we believe what they say because they have been shown to be truthful, we believe they stand behind their actions and take responsibility for them, and in general we'd love to have them on our side. While people of integrity may seem to have emerged as fully developed humans with that trait, in reality our perception of their integrity has been built piece by piece over many years of observation.

A reputation for integrity used to be a prerequisite for a successful politician or government official. Sadly, in some cases those standards seem to have dropped, but they must be reinstated. The three people we'll look at next, Daniel Patrick Moynihan, Margaret Thatcher, and Paul Volcker, in different roles and in different eras, embodied integrity in all they said and did. What shaped these leaders and what drove their characters?

Daniel Patrick Moynihan

Everyone is entitled to his own opinion, but not his own facts.

—Daniel Patrick Moynihan

Daniel Patrick Moynihan was a larger-than-life public intellectual, the embodiment of a senator who might have been as at home in the ancient Roman senate as he was in the U.S. Senate. His career as ambassador to India, as ambassador to the United Nations, and as senator was based almost entirely on integrity. He meant what he said and lived according to a set of moral codes. Since he left the Senate in 2001, there have been precious few of his stature in that body.

He was born in Tulsa, Oklahoma, in 1927, but his family soon moved to New York. After graduating from Tufts University, he worked for New York governor W. Averell Harriman and in the Kennedy and Johnson Labor departments before leaving government to teach at Harvard. He returned as a counselor to President Richard Nixon and was later named ambassador to India and then to the UN before winning a Senate seat from New York in 1976.

He was a logical and erudite speaker, above all interested in delivering a clear view of the United States, warts and all, whether speaking in Delhi, at the UN, or in the Bronx.

"Am I embarrassed to speak for a less than perfect democracy? Not one bit. Find me a better one. Do I suppose there are societies which are free of sin? No, I don't. Do I think ours is, on balance, incomparably the most hopeful set of human relations the world has? Yes, I do."

Nobody did it better.

Armed with a PhD from Tufts (as well as a degree from the London School of Economics), Moynihan was well positioned to know what he was talking about.

He was a great believer in government transparency. He was

pretty much a free-speech and free-press absolutist, positions that pair with his views on transparency. In his 1971 essay "The Presidency and the Press," Moynihan took note of the local press as a barometer of the political nature of a regime. Local papers filled with bad news are indicative of a libertarian society. But a press filled with good news means jails are filled with good people.

A free press will report all the news, not just what the government may want—or not want—the populace to know. An independent press is crucial to a democracy. Similarly, citizens have the right to free speech (part of the First Amendment to our Constitution), which means they can criticize government without fear of retribution. Or at least that's what it should mean. Modern interpretations extend free speech to also mean free expression, such as wearing T-shirts with offensive slogans or burning an American flag, as distasteful as that may be to others.

Moynihan's political analysis was most often on the mark, including this prescient quote from his 1993 book, *Pandaemonium*: "The Soviet Union came apart along ethnic lines. The most important factor in this breakup was the disinclination of Slavic Ukraine to continue under a regime dominated by Slavic Russia." The clash between Serbia and Croatia led to the breakup of Yugoslavia, though they had only small differences in genealogy and a nearly common language.

In the Senate, he long championed rail transportation, and the train hall next to Penn Station is named for him, as is the U.S. District Courthouse in Foley Square in New York.

When the Moynihan Train Hall opened on January 1, 2021, it represented a long-held dream of the late senator. It replaced the old post office building between Eighth and Ninth Avenues and Thirty-First and Thirty-Third Streets in Manhattan, across the street from Madison Square Garden and the rest of Pennsylvania Station, to which it connects. It features a graceful Beaux Arts facade and offers easier access to Amtrak, New Jersey Transit, and Long Island Railroad passengers, although at the time of this writing they still have to contend with less-than-ideal conditions in Penn Station itself. And Senator Moynihan's monument could probably use a few more benches for commuters.

I would like to focus on a speech he gave to the UN General Assembly in 1975, while he was the U.S. ambassador.

The UN speech is not only a remarkable defense of Israel against the charge that their conduct regarding Palestinians was racist but also an argument for realism and integrity. It could well have been pulled from today's headlines. It would do us all good if more people heeded its lessons.

Its crux: "The United States rises to declare before the General Assembly of the United Nations, and before the world, that it does not acknowledge, it will not abide by, it will never acquiesce in this infamous act" of declaring Israel to be a racist country.

There is nothing like plain language to win an argument. There's no doubt about what he means.

The United Nations General Assembly adopted Resolution 3379 in a vote of 72–35 with 32 abstentions. It equates anti-Zionism with racism.

Moynihan's legacy is his eloquence in defense of freedom. His words could, and probably should, be echoed today. The world would be a better place.

Lessons

Daniel Patrick Moynihan's distinguished career as a diplomat and senator was based squarely on his ability to project integrity with every word he said. That's a lesson for us all.

- The best way to display integrity is to tell the truth fully, plainly, and, if possible, eloquently.
- Scorn for an opponent's argument should be used sparingly. Facts are better.
- As the man said, you're entitled to your own opinion—that's free speech—but not your own facts. Know what you are talking about.

Margaret Thatcher

The lady's not for turning.

—Margaret Thatcher

Margaret Thatcher was tough. I once ran into her in Hamleys, the famous toy shop in London, when one of my then small sons was making a bit of a racket over some toy. I heard a booming voice: "This is not America. Make your kids behave." It was Mrs. Thatcher.

A colleague who as a reporter interviewed her many times recalls that when she didn't like a particular question, she would say: "That's not the question to ask. This is the question to ask," and then she'd answer her own, always more congenial, question.

Her integrity showed up in her loyalty to allies, in her consistency in outlook, and in her firmness in command. It was no accident that the Soviets dubbed her the Iron Lady (a nickname she enjoyed).

When in 1979, the first year of her premiership, her economic policies made things worse before she was sure they'd get better, with unemployment doubling, even some Conservative Party colleagues urged her to do a U-turn and loosen up. "The lady's not for turning," she told the Tory Party Conference in 1980.

She would survive an IRA bomb in Brighton in 1984 that killed five people, including one of her closest advisers, and wounded another fifteen. During a 1988 salmonella scare, she appeared at the doorway of 10 Downing Street to tell the assembled reporters that she had just had scrambled eggs on toast for lunch, and "I quite enjoyed it."

The Iron Lady's steadfast rejection of the then Soviet Union, alongside her firm ally and friend Ronald Reagan, helped millions of Eastern Europeans shed the Soviet yoke. Few Western politicians (Reagan excepted) combined her moral clarity and communication skills on this topic.

Margaret Roberts was born in Grantham, England, in 1925. Her father was a grocer and later mayor of the town. She studied chemistry at Oxford and was president of the Oxford University Conservative Association. She worked as a research chemist while studying law, became a barrister in 1954, and won a seat in Parliament representing Finchley in 1959 on her second try.

Thatcher (who had married Denis Thatcher in 1951) served as secretary of state for education and science in the Edward Heath government, famously ending a school milk program, earning her the sobriquet "Maggie Thatcher, milk snatcher" from political opponents.

After Heath lost two elections to Harold Wilson in 1974, Thatcher was the only major Tory figure willing to challenge him for the party leadership, which she won in 1975 by consolidating the right wing of the party. After four years in opposition, she defeated Wilson's successor, James Callaghan, in the 1979 general election. Her victory came amid disastrous scenes for Labour of long unemployment lines and garbage piling up in the streets of London. She would go on to win two more elections, serving eleven years, the longest stretch in office for any prime minister since the nineteenth century.

Margaret Thatcher was a firm European on economic matters, believing that the EU benefited Britain as long as she could extract what she felt was Britain's "fair share" of farm and industrial subsidies and budget contributions. She often infuriated her French and German counterparts, among others, by fiercely opposing the "ever closer political union" they espoused, frequently holding up EU summit negotiations into the wee hours. A friend who covered many of these meetings recalls he asked a French spokesman at one a.m. how long the meeting was likely to continue. "Until Mrs. Thatcher gets tired," he replied wearily. But she would never have backed Brexit, the 2016 referendum that ultimately took the U.K. out of the EU. For one thing, she detested referenda, feeling political leaders were elected to lead, and for another, she thought Britain was better off staying in and fighting for its interests, rather than negotiating from the outside. As of this writing, it looks like she was correct, as few benefits of Brexit have appeared during a bad economic downturn.

Her unstinting belief in the power of individuals to change their own lives, rather than depend on the government (akin to the U.S. GOP under Reagan), completely changed a Britain that still seemed to cling to the remnants of postwar state ownership and generous subsidies for dying industries such as steelmaking and coal mining. She was one of the first popularizers of the idea of small government, far from an accepted idea in the U.K. at the time.

Ronald Reagan fired more than eleven thousand air-traffic controllers in 1981, breaking the PATCO union and seriously diluting union power in the U.S. Margaret Thatcher's opportunity to beat the power of U.K. unions came three years later, when the U.K. National Union of Mineworkers, led by Arthur Scargill, struck the National Coal Board, halting much but not all coal production. The Thatcher government reacted to the closures and picketing by using the police to break up the miners' demonstrations. A journalist friend who covered the yearlong strike tells me it was extremely divisive and sometimes violent. Thatcher wouldn't budge, though, and eventually the strike was ruled illegal because Scargill had never taken a national vote of his members, and it ended. Of the 175 working coal pits in 1983, all are now closed. Strikes, which had plagued the Labour Government Thatcher had beaten in 1979, all but disappeared.

A measure of Mrs. Thatcher's integrity, which made her arguably the most admired U.K. prime minister after Winston Churchill (see chapter 6) was that the lady really wasn't for turning. Whether privatizing nationalized companies or freeing up the housing market by selling off many of the government-owned council houses that dominated the landscape or taking on the powerful coal miners' union or fighting interminably at summit meetings for Britain's interests within the EU or going to war with Argentina over the Falkland Islands, Mrs. Thatcher never really changed. She might compromise on some details, but not on what she considered matters of principle. That's integrity.

Her philosophy was often dubbed "neoliberalism," after the ideas of Friedrich Hayek, whom Thatcher often quoted, with the liberal part taking on its meaning from the nineteenth-century idea of free-market capitalism. There's nothing liberal about it in the American sense.

Political commentators dubbed the philosophy Thatcherism and her followers Thatcherites, even after she left office. Two of her successors as Tory prime ministers, John Major and David Cameron, were mostly Thatcherites. Boris Johnson less so.

In a very revealing lecture given in honor of her late friend and colleague Sir Keith Joseph in 1996, she called integrity an old-fashioned word.

"But, for a politician, integrity is everything," she said.

"In politics, integrity really lies in the conviction that it's only on the basis of truth that power should be won—or indeed can be *worth* winning. It lies in an unswerving belief that you have to be *right*."

While she was discussing her colleague in that speech, she was aptly describing herself.

She often called herself a "conviction politician," meaning that she would stick to her guns, explain her actions and reasoning, and trust in the voters.

In a speech she gave to the Centre for Policy Studies in 1988, in the middle of her premiership, Thatcher both summed up her philosophy and revealed a lot about her character.

In plain talk, she described individualism and defended it from critics who called it selfish and materialistic. More people should take responsibility for looking after their families, she said, rather than expect others to do so. It is not selfish to have ambition, to benefit financially from your efforts.

Thatcherism, economically, meant tax cuts, privatizing nationalized industries, and trimming government spending, with the one exception of the popular National Health Service, which all British factions seem to compete to spend more on before every election. Still, she was firmly a capitalist.

Her long-serving chancellor of the exchequer (equivalent to the U.S. treasury secretary), Nigel Lawson (father of the TV chef Nigella Lawson), said Thatcherism consisted of "free markets, financial discipline, firm control over public expenditure, tax cuts, nationalism, and 'Victorian values,' privatization, and a dash of populism."

It wasn't always popular. Some privatizations were criticized as giveaways to friendly businessmen. Her idea of a poll tax, or a same flat-rate charge regardless of income to replace property taxes, led to riots in London and elsewhere and was abolished and replaced by a council tax that returned to variable rates depending on house size and value. The miners' strike was divisive.

In foreign policy, Thatcherism entailed a fierce British nationalism, unwavering support for NATO, an Extra Special Relationship with the United States, and a firm rejection of communism in the Soviet Union, China, and everywhere else. The nationalism part entailed curbs on inward immigration.

A recession in the late 1980s led to high unemployment and business failures. After eleven years in office, even close Thatcher allies like Sir Geoffrey Howe and Michael Heseltine turned against her. She was basically forced to resign in 1990 and was ennobled by Queen Elizabeth II as Baroness Thatcher of Kesteven; and while she was entitled to sit in the House of Lords, she rarely did. She died after a long illness, out of the public lime-light, in 2013.

The close political ties between the U.K. and U.S., especially after World War II, were often called the Special Relation-ship. But the ideological ties between Ronald Reagan and Margaret Thatcher in the 1980s came to be known as the Extra Special Relationship and were the subject of a TV miniseries and several books. Both conservative, both at odds with unions at home and the Soviet Union abroad, the two leaders met often and cheerfully. Little could shake their friendship. A journalist friend of mine recalls doing an inter-view with Mrs. Thatcher in 10 Downing Street, during which she voiced some criticism of U.S. policy. The reporter later asked Reagan, at a summit meeting, whether he agreed with this criticism. "I never have any problem with my friend Mar-garet Thatcher," he replied. The relationship was strained during the Falklands War, when the U.S. publicly stayed out of the battle between the U.K. and Argentina over the is-lands, and the U.S. later sold arms to Argentina over U.K. objections. Thatcher sent a very strong diplomatic note to the U.S. Reagan's reported reply: "Well, that's Maggie."

Having traveled all over the U.K. before, during, and after Thatcher's premiership, I can testify to the magnitude of the change. Not everything came directly from her policies, of course, but the miracle of the free market has led to a generally modernized economy, with flourishing shops and many fine restaurants serving all types of cuisine, the latter fact being a huge change from the early 1970s. Even Tony Blair, the long-serving Labour prime minister, kept most of her reforms and conceded they were necessary to modernize Britain.

It's a tribute to her integrity that Thatcherism, like Reagan-omics in the U.S., has embodied a philosophy, and is a term used by both opponents and proponents. I don't have anything like that named after me. Do you?

Lessons

Through integrity and passion, Margaret Thatcher changed Britain in many ways, offering many lessons:

- Don't be "for turning." When you feel you are right, defend your ideas.
- Don't allow self-confidence to turn into arrogance. State your case firmly and clearly, without snide remarks or condescension.
- Never give up on core fundamentals. It took Mrs. Thatcher a decade to see some of her ideas, like the poll tax, implemented.

Paul Volcker

What's the subject of life—to get rich? All of those fellows out there getting rich could be dancing around the real subject of life.

—Paul Volcker

Like Stephen Hawking in chapter 4, Paul Volcker opens the introduction to his last book with another of my favorite jokes.

To paraphrase: A man goes into a pet store to buy a parrot. The first one he sees is a fine bird, and the shopkeeper says he costs five thousand dollars. Why so much? The bird speaks

English, French, German, Italian, and Spanish. Perfect to deal with the EU. Don't care. How much is that one over there? Ten thousand. Ten thousand? He speaks Mandarin, Cantonese, Japanese, and is working on Korean. Perfect for emerging Asia. Don't care. He points at a glassy-eyed bird whose feathers are all falling out. I'll take that one. How much? Twenty-five thousand. What? What's so special about him? Says the shop-keeper: "I don't know, but the other two call him chairman."

Paul Volcker was pretty much called chairman by everyone long after his tenure as chairman of the Federal Reserve Board from 1979 to 1987. At a husky six feet seven, he stood out from most crowds, and with his bald head and ever-present cigar, he became one of the best-known public figures of the 1980s. Appearances aside, Volcker's reputation for integrity came from his fighting, and eventually taming, the runaway inflation he inherited. When the 2007–2008 financial crisis came along two decades later, he was the natural choice to help write new rules to prevent a repetition.

I was fortunate to share a dinner table with him on several occasions. Even when the party contained the likes of Henry Kaufman, the famous Wall Street economist whose interest rate predictions moved markets and who was sometimes called Dr. Doom, the room always hushed in deference when Volcker spoke.

Paul Volcker seemed to have chosen his path fairly early, writing his senior thesis at Princeton in 1949 on the Federal Reserve. He joined the New York Fed as a junior economist in 1952, leaving briefly for Chase Bank in 1957 before joining the Treasury Department in the Kennedy administration in 1962. He rejoined Chase in 1965 but four years later returned to the Treasury. He was named president of the New York Fed in 1975, putting him on the Fed's board, and was appointed chairman in 1979 by President Jimmy Carter; he would be reappointed by President Ronald Reagan in 1983.

His term at the Fed was fraught as he battled the worst bout of inflation since World War II. When he took over in 1979, the country was still reeling from OPEC oil price hikes, and inflation, which had hit 12.2 percent in 1974 before subsiding, was on its way back up to pass that mark, reaching 13.3 percent in 1979 and topping out at 13.5 percent in 1980.

Volcker's response was to hike interest rates, around 11 percent when he became chairman, to a stratospheric 20 percent in June 1981. The medicine was harsh: The economy plunged into recession and unemployment rose to more than 10 percent as companies unable to afford to borrow had to cut staff or close. The Dow Jones Industrial Average plunged by nearly 30 percent from late 1980 to mid-1982.

Volcker wasn't surprised. "Knowing something and acting on that knowledge in a political setting are two different things. . . . Finally, the markets come and hit you over the head."

Inflation is the rate at which prices rise in an economy, usually measured by a basket of goods and services. Inflation decreases the purchasing power of consumers but increases the value of some assets. It can be caused by an oversupply of government-created money accompanied by rises in prices for commodities such as food and energy. Inflation is usually fought by central banks like the Fed raising interest rates to make borrowing more money or taking out a mortgage, for example, more expensive. So-called hyperinflation, with rates exceeding 50 percent a month, in some cases, has afflicted economies from the Weimar Republic in post–World War I Germany to Hungary after World War II to Yugoslavia in the 1990s to Zimbabwe in 2007. Higher interest rates may slow the economy so much that it tips into negative growth, which if prolonged is called a recession. Most severe bouts of inflation end in a recession or, in some cases, a depression.

But it worked. By 1983, inflation was below 4 percent, but unemployment was still high, at over 6 percent.

Reflecting later on the situation, Volcker called double-digit inflation a "terrible thing," but it created a sense of urgency to take more forceful measures.

When President Carter was considering Volcker for the job in 1979, the central banker was characteristically blunt: "If you appoint me, I will raise interest rates and choke off the inflation, and that will have bad political repercussions for you." Indeed, in part because of the economy, and in part because of the Iran hostage crisis, Jimmy Carter lost his reelection bid in 1980 to Ronald Reagan.

That Paul Volcker could maintain both his reputation and his integrity during this tumultuous time is a sign of character. He was pretty much detested by everyone—people sent him their car keys saying they couldn't afford their car payments; a builder sent him a two-by-four inscribed in Sharpie: Please lower these insane interest rates. Volcker kept the two-by-four in his office after he left the Fed.

Still, Volcker persisted, saying backing down too early would have been worse. It would just put off the day of reckoning.

Not only did Volcker's reputation survive intact after the economy recovered but it also seemed to take on mythic proportions. When the Great Recession hit in 2007–2008, it was natural that President Barack Obama named the man who tamed inflation the chairman of a newly created Economic Recovery Advisory Board.

Volcker's work on this board, which examined the banking crisis—largely caused by the collapse in the market for questionable bundles of loans tied to mortgages—and suggested legislative remedies, helped shaped the Dodd-Frank Wall Street Reform and Consumer Protection Act of 2010, which contained the Volcker Rule. The banks hated it and it was later modified, but Volcker always stood by it, even though after all the Congressional sausage making, he said he would have preferred a simpler bill with more direct enforcement.

The so-called Volcker Rule, originally part of the Dodd-Frank Wall Street Reform and Consumer Protection Act of 2010, generally prohibits banks from using deposits to trade for their own benefit. Formulated by Paul Volcker long after his term as Federal Reserve chairman, it went through a series of changes, and in 2020 it was amended to allow banks to invest in certain instruments such as securitized loans. The rule drew great fire from banks and is still regarded as the major reform enacted after the 2007–2008 financial crisis, which brought down Lehman Brothers and many other institutions.

Somewhat bemused by his celebrity, Volcker delivered a lecture in 1990 entitled "The Triumph of Central Banking?" (Note the question mark.)

Central bankerly qualities—restraint, continuity, prudence—have come to be in style. Price stability as the principal goal of monetary policy was previously foreign to the earlier postwar generation, he said.

Then he boldly posited that when central banks succeed with price and financial stability, it could be time to talk about merging independent monetary authorities into a central bank to preserve a stable common currency. He knew that was unlikely in his lifetime.

At his death in 2019, what stood out in all the obituaries and tributes was a universal recognition of his integrity. It would have been much tougher to tame inflation in the 1980s without Volcker's integrity at the helm and much harder to learn the lessons of what to do when inflation reappears.

Lessons

Paul Volcker commanded every room he entered. His life offers lessons on how to do the same.

- Always explain, never complain.
- Authority comes from backing up your words with actions that work.
- Be aware of opposing opinions—such as a two-by-four delivered to your office—but stick to your guns if you're convinced you are right.
- Politics—be they internal company or national politics—can make life miserable. Carry on through them.

Chapter Nine

TRANSPARENCY

Whoever is careless with the truth in small matters cannot be trusted with important matters.

—Albert Einstein

There's an old computer acronym, WYSIWYG, standing for "what you see is what you get," generally meaning the display on a screen. In people's behavior, WYSIWYG too often doesn't apply. People shade the truth, sometimes aren't what they seem, or prove unreliable in a crisis. But when we do see what we get, we regard that person as being transparent. This is another character trait worth examining and pursuing.

Transparency is different from honesty, although honesty is a good character trait to have as well. Transparency is sort of projected honesty, making people feel confident that a person is telling the truth and has nothing to hide.

Our three subjects, Katharine Graham, Jimmy Stewart, and Father Theodore Hesburgh, all displayed transparency in their own ways. Katharine Graham withstood massive pressure and allowed her journalists to print the truth even when high government officials tried to stop them. Actor Stewart played good guys in the movies and was a good guy in real life. Theodore Hesburgh inspired thousands of students at Notre Dame and millions beyond those walls.

If you don't lead your life transparently, you'll find it difficult to develop a sound, respected character.

Katharine Graham

> Go ahead, go ahead, go ahead. Let's go. Let's publish.
> —Katharine Graham

Katharine Graham to me is the perfect example of how integrity and tenacity served the cause of transparency through the news media. Regrettably, she may have been the last of a breed of fearless news executives devoted solely to the cause of maintaining the free and vigorous press that is the cornerstone of our democracy.

Graham became publisher of the *Washington Post* through the tragic suicide of her husband, but it was her transparency and integrity in the job that carried the *Post* through two major publishing challenges to the government—the *Pentagon Papers* and Watergate—as well as building the *Post* into one of the most financially solid and influential newspapers in the country at the time. Her autobiography, *Personal History* (Vintage, 1997), won a Pulitzer Prize, making her the rare publisher to have done so. (I can think only of Peter Kann of the *Wall Street Journal*, but perhaps there are others.)

Katharine Meyer was born in 1917 into a prominent New York family. Her father, Eugene, was a financier and chairman of the Federal Reserve (see chapter 8) who bought the *Post* at a bankruptcy sale in 1933. Her mother, Agnes, a bohemian artist type, knew everyone from Gertrude Stein to Picasso to the philosopher John Dewey to Georgia O'Keeffe to Thomas Mann to Eleanor Roosevelt (see chapter 7).

Katharine attended Vassar College and the University of Chicago and worked as a reporter in San Francisco before joining her father's paper back in Washington for $25 a week in the letters to the editor department. She never left. She married

Philip Graham in 1940. He became the publisher of the *Post* in 1946.

As she recounts in her book, the Grahams were a true Washington power couple, entertaining the Kennedys, Johnsons, Kissingers, Reagans, Buffetts, and the media establishment. In 1960, Philip Graham was instrumental in getting John F. Kennedy to pick Lyndon Johnson as his running mate.

She loved it. Washington, she said, offered more different kinds of people than she otherwise could have known. "In Washington, the public and the private intertwine in such a way that they can't be easily separated. This is the city where the personal and the political are most closely linked."

Katharine became publisher of the *Post* after Philip died by suicide in 1963, after years of growing mental illness. She held that position for sixteen years.

She always knew and respected the power the *Post* had; what it published mattered. The paper couldn't just follow events—it had the power to set agendas.

While she worked steadily to shore up the paper's finances, her first big journalism test came in 1971. While the *New York Times* was the first to publish extracts from the *Pentagon Papers*, a secret report leaked by Daniel Ellsberg, a U.S. military analyst and economist, which showed big mistakes in the country's war effort in Vietnam, the *Post* had also obtained a copy. Editors led by Ben Bradlee were debating whether to publish it in defiance of a court order that had halted the *Times*'s publication after one article. Bradlee called Graham, who was in the middle of a party at her home, and told her the editors wanted to publish and the lawyers advised against. "Go ahead, go ahead, go ahead. Let's go. Let's publish," she said. And she later said: "The only way to assert the right to publish is to publish."

It took courage to stand up to the government and fight for the First Amendment, which protects freedom of the press. It also took conviction on Graham's part, and the newspaper's editors and reporters, to let the public know the truth about the war. The Supreme Court eventually agreed and lifted the tem-

porary injunction against the *New York Times* with Justice Hugo
Black saying the press had the right to "bare the secrets of gov-
ernment and inform the people." Forty years later, the *Pentagon
Papers* were declassified.

Graham's attitude remained the same a year later when news
of Watergate broke. Initially it was dismissed as a "third-rate
burglary" at the Democratic National Committee offices. But
pursued relentlessly by *Post* reporters Bob Woodward and Carl
Bernstein, the scandal eventually led to President Richard
Nixon's resignation from office and propelled thousands of idealistic youngsters to journalism school.

Watergate became an iconic feat of newspaper reporting by
Carl Bernstein and Bob Woodward, as recounted in the
book and the 1976 movie *All the President's Men*. Graham's
character doesn't appear on-screen, at her request; her
character does appear in the 2017 movie about the *Pentagon
Papers*, *The Post*, with Graham played by Meryl Streep. The
movie also immortalized the character of Deep Throat,
Woodward and Bernstein's secret source, played by Hal
Holbrook and ultimately revealed to be Deputy FBI Director
Mark Felt.

Graham's role in Watergate was key. Under immense political pressure and facing legal liability, she backed Woodward,
Bernstein, Ben Bradlee, and other *Post* reporters and editors un-
flinchingly. She downplayed her role as behind the scenes,
though asking devil's advocate–type questions to make sure the
stories were "fair, factual, and accurate." If so, there was no
chance a story would be held or spiked (a journalism term for
"killed") no matter the stakes or consequences.

"I have often been credited with courage for backing our editors in Watergate," she wrote in *Personal History*. "The truth is

that I never felt there was much choice. . . . Courage applies when one has a choice."

I beg to differ. Doing what she did in both cases required immense courage, fueled by a strong belief in our government system and our free press.

If the *Post* had stopped with the Watergate break-in and not followed the shocking facts that led to the indictment of sixty-nine government officials (forty-eight of whom were convicted) and ultimately toppled the president from power, then the paper would have been denying the public knowledge about the gross misuse of the institution.

Nixon and his cronies never forgave her.

The concept that editors have autonomy—free from government influence—was key for her. Reflecting on a quote to that point, she said: "News is what someone wants suppressed. Everything else is advertising. . . . Democracy depends on information circulating freely in society."

Post editors in 2017 would adapt this phrase somewhat to "Democracy Dies in Darkness" and put it in the masthead.

Graham was never completely comfortable with the legacy of Watergate. She worried that idealistic young people would want to investigate everything and overdo it. Be skeptical, yes, but not vengeful. Above all, be fair.

She accepted that some government secrets need to be kept, and that the *Post* did keep them when appropriate. What was important was that the press, not the government, got to decide whether to print what it knew.

Despite the renown of the *Pentagon Papers* and Watergate, the *Post* financially was on shaky ground. Graham herself said she faced a steep learning curve on the business side. In the early 1970s, the newspaper industry was facing challenges from television and would later be hit by the digital revolution. Graham, with help from early investor Warren Buffett, steadied the ship by investments in, among other things, television. Her son Donald took over from her as publisher in 1979 and greatly improved the *Post*'s finances. The Graham family sold the *Post* to Amazon Inc. founder Jeff Bezos in 2013.

The mere fact that the *Washington Post* remains one of the most influential and successful newspapers in the country today isn't just because of Jeff Bezos's backing, though that helps.

More important, it seems to me, is the journalistic independence that's in its lifeblood, and which was largely put there by Katharine Graham.

Lessons

Katharine Graham's life was one of constantly learning lessons and applying them to aid transparency and the free press.

- Transparency is a virtue unto itself, leading to honesty and integrity.
- Truth-telling can be hard and sometimes costly, but it's always worth it.
- The backing of the top boss, even if it's in the shadows, is the most powerful motivational tool in any organization.

Jimmy Stewart

A James Stewart picture must have two vital ingredients; it will be clean and it will involve the triumph of the underdog over the bully.

—Jimmy Stewart

A friend tells this story about Jimmy Stewart, which displays the humility and grounding that's evident in both his military and Hollywood careers. Mr. Stewart and his wife were dropping off their daughter at college for her freshman year in 1969. The roommate's father, not a movie fan, didn't recognize the world-famous star. "Hi, I'm Joe Smith. I'm in groceries. What's your line?" Neither fazed nor embarrassed, Stewart replied: "Uhh, James Stewart. I'm in show business."

To hark back to the opening of this chapter, WYSIWYG, what you see is what you got with Jimmy Stewart. His currency was an authenticity impossible to fake, and very rarely equaled.

In the 1939 Frank Capra classic, *Mr. Smith Goes to Washington*, Jimmy Stewart plays Jefferson Smith, who gets appointed to the Senate, soon gets a dose of potential corruption, and leads a talking filibuster on the Senate floor, rare even for 1939 and a lost art now. I've always enjoyed this movie—it has many memorable lines. But during my lifetime there have been few real-life senators who have lived up to the ideals of this fictional one. Three are in this book: Daniel Patrick Moynihan, John McCain, and Margaret Chase Smith. (Abe Lincoln would qualify, but he was never a senator.)

Stewart was whom he played in the movies—decent, morally centered, down-to-earth with no airs. It's no wonder *It's a Wonderful Life* was his favorite film and also Frank Capra's.

He would walk his and his wife Gloria's two dogs, Beau and Simba, on his own. Tourist buses would come by on Hollywood home tours, and instead of dashing to the back or diving into the garage, he would chat with the tourists. They had a very nice white frame house, not a mansion, in Beverly Hills with a pool and Rolls-Royce in the driveway. The Oscar for *The Philadelphia Story* was in the den.

On the corner next to their home, there was an elaborate Moroccan mansion. When Stewart bought it, the owner and the neighbor said something along the lines of "Great to see you're moving out of that house of yours." In fact, Stewart planned to tear it down so that the dogs would have more room to play.

Stewart loved his dogs. He even read a poem he had written

for Beau, on the Johnny Carson show in July 1981; Carson was reduced to tears.

In the 1930s, a bunch of models from New York were flown out to LA to be in the movies. One was Stewart's future wife, Gloria, who with another model went on a double date with Stewart and his best friend, Henry Fonda. The women obviously got dressed to the nines. Stewart and Fonda drove them out to the middle of the desert and flew model airplanes.

Stewart was not loquacious, but when he said something, it was great. A friend tells me the story of having lunch with him in New York when Stewart was starring in a Broadway revival of *Harvey*, the wonderful play and movie about an invisible rabbit and his best friend. His stepson worked at Dillon, Read & Co. and the lunch was in the executive dining room. After lunch, the stepson was going to take Stewart down to the trading floor of the NYSE. His daughter asked: "So you're going to go down on the floor?" He responded: "I wasn't planning to drink that much!" That was pretty much all he said during the lunch, letting his wife and daughter speak for him.

Jimmy Stewart got a degree in architecture from Princeton in 1932 and joined a summer stock company in Falmouth, Massachusetts, where he met his lifelong friend Henry Fonda. A few undistinguished Broadway plays led to a movie contract from MGM in 1934. Stewart appeared with Spencer Tracy in *The Murder Man* in 1935. There followed a succession of classics, including *You Can't Take It with You*, *Mr. Smith Goes to Washington*, and *The Philadelphia Story*.

Stewart enlisted in the Army in 1941, a few months before the Japanese bombed Pearl Harbor. Since he was already an accomplished amateur pilot, he joined the Army Air Corps and wound up flying more than twenty bomber missions. He earned the Distinguished Flying Cross, the Air Medal, and the French Croix de Guerre. He remained in the Army Reserves and was promoted to brigadier general in 1959.

After the war, Stewart resumed his Hollywood career, and his first film was Frank Capra's *It's a Wonderful Life,* followed by a bunch of Alfred Hitchcock classics, including *Rear Window*, *Vertigo*, and *The Man Who Knew Too Much*. His character's most famous speech in *It's a Wonderful Life*, in which he defended and dignified the "rabble" of working people, neatly sums up Stewarts's humanity. Think about the message the next time you watch the movie. It's a must-watch every holiday in our home.

> In addition to Stewart, celebrities who served in World War II included Ted Williams, Joe DiMaggio, Yogi Berra, Joe Lewis, Clark Gable, Paul Newman, Kirk Douglas, and Clint Eastwood, among others. Many were, like Stewart, pilots; some held down desk jobs; but all contributed to the war effort and to public morale at home.

Ronald Reagan gave Stewart the Presidential Medal of Freedom in 1995 on the same day as Mother Teresa, along with a few others, such as Frank Sinatra and General Charles E. Yeager, the Air Force test pilot who was the first to travel at the speed of sound. That must have been quite a ceremony!

Jimmy Stewart continued to delight audiences in the movie and TV industries, as well as the occasional tourist on Hollywood homes of the stars bus tours. He died in 1997 at the age of eighty-nine.

Lessons

What you saw on-screen with Jimmy Stewart was what you got in real life. There are lessons in that.

- Transparency is closely related to honesty and integrity. WYSIWYG.
- Friends say Jimmy Stewart was the same on-screen and off, walking the dogs, eating lunch on Wall Street, flying

model airplanes with Henry Fonda, or accepting a medal
from fellow actor Ronald Reagan. That's transparency—
and character.
- Bring the same temperament to everything you do, be it
acting or flying a jet bomber.
- When you achieve fame, don't let it go to your head.
- Remember the dignity of the "rabble."

Theodore Hesburgh

The very essence of leadership is that you have to have
vision. You can't blow an uncertain trumpet.

—Theodore Hesburgh

Theodore Hesburgh, known to many as Father Ted, blew a
very certain trumpet as president of the University of Notre
Dame for thirty-five years; exerted a compelling moral force on
all who interacted with him; was a human and civil rights
leader; was awarded the Presidential Medal of Freedom (in
1964); and probably holds the record for most honorary degrees, with more than 150.

From a school primarily known for Knute Rockne and the
football team, Hesburgh turned Notre Dame into the interna-
tionally acclaimed, co-educational university it is today. Yes,
they still play football. Both during and after that long tenure,
Hesburgh was a trusted adviser to presidents and civil rights
leaders, from Lyndon Johnson to Barack Obama and Dr. Martin Luther King Jr. to Al Sharpton.

I had many encounters with Father Ted.

The initial one was my first day as a freshman at Notre Dame.
The entire class was assembled at "the Grotto," the on-campus
shrine to Our Lady of Lourdes. Hesburgh asked each of us to
look to the left, then to the right, and he told us that in twelve
months most of these people would be gone, because the aca-

demics were so tough and the chaff got winnowed out. He was right.

Hesburgh never put on airs when dealing with students. He would often take his place in the cafeteria line, fill his tray, and come sit with us at the long wooden tables. As we chatted, he usually complained about the food, saying, "I'm not sure we should eat this." But we all did.

As he was preparing to step down as president, and I was well into my career, we met in the Basilica of the Sacred Heart on campus, along with Father Edmund Joyce, his executive vice president and number two guy. He asked me what I thought he should do next. I replied: "You and Ned should hop in a car, drive across the country, and write a book about it." They did. *Travels with Ted and Ned* is well worth looking up.

Theodore Hesburgh was born in Syracuse, New York, in 1917, and has said that he wanted to be a priest from the age of six. He had a thoroughly Catholic education, from high school through to the Pontifical Gregorian University in Rome to Holy Cross and the Catholic University of America.

He often said that as soon as he became conscious, he would need to choose what he wanted to become in life; he knew he wanted to become a priest.

He began teaching at Notre Dame in 1945, and was named head of the Theology Department in 1948, executive vice president in 1949, and president in 1952. You could say that was a meteoric rise.

Under Hesburgh's leadership, Notre Dame expanded its academic quality, attracting more than one hundred new distinguished professorships; built or refurbished more than forty buildings; increased the endowment from $9 million to $350 million; and doubled its enrollment to nearly ten thousand, including women, beginning in 1972. He transitioned Notre Dame from the religious leadership of the Congregation of the Holy Cross and transferred governance to a board of lay and religious leaders, all the while insisting on academic independence.

Mainly, though, on the shoulders of Hesburgh's transparency and integrity, Notre Dame emerged as a great university. He was a visible embodiment of the highest ideals on and off campus, a true moral force to be reckoned with.

He, or any university president, had a special duty to be "an apostle of freedom," defending academic freedom and truth against any who questioned them. Philosophers and scientists may clash, but they don't clash over what is true. Universities, and I can declare this was true at Notre Dame, need to treat all knowledge as legitimate if it is derived through faithful research. Hesburgh made it his life's work to ensure Notre Dame would have the finest research and teaching talent not only in physics and chemistry and biology but also in art and literature, for all these disciplines make a well-rounded person.

He also thought physical activity and sports—especially football—were important. Football clearly held a special place for him; in a speech as early as 1952 he reflected on the game and its players and life.

He emphasized development of the mind and the spirit, not just the body. At Notre Dame, he said, playing a sport comes as a supplement, rather than as a substitute, for a great education and the development of moral character. It sets the stage for young men to work as intelligently and honestly in their professional lives—and personal lives, for that matter—as they did on the playing field. These values are the bedrock of good character. Father Hesburgh both embodied them and made it his life's work to pass them on to his students and a wider audience.

Hesburgh was particularly keen on academic improvement, even as football fortunes waxed and waned. The 1953 Fighting Irish went undefeated, and the football team won national titles in 1964, 1966, 1973, 1977, and 1988. In between were many lean years. Notre Dame didn't go to bowl games starting in 1925, calling them "glorified exhibitions." Hesburgh took them back to the Cotton Bowl in 1970 in order to use the prize money for academic scholarships. They beat the Texas Longhorns and have been back to many bowls since.

College football was king at Notre Dame long before Hesburgh's time. The legendary coach Knute Rockne led the Fighting Irish (the origin of the nickname is unclear) between 1918 and 1930 to three national championships. Rockne was immortalized in the 1940 movie *Knute Rockne, All-American*, in which he was played by Pat O'Brien. He asks his team to "Win one for the Gipper," referring to the deathbed request of George Gipp, who is played by Ronald Reagan. The 77,000-capacity Notre Dame Stadium, built in 1930 under Rockne's guidance, is often called "the house that Rockne built."

Hesburgh used his pulpit at Notre Dame and his reputation for honesty and transparency to promote civil rights during its most tumultuous era. He served on the U.S. Civil Rights Commission from 1957 to 1972, as chairman the final three years. He spoke at a rally led by Dr. Martin Luther King Jr. in Chicago in 1964, as well as at many other such appearances.

Hesburgh once explained his work on civil rights as fundamental to his faith. In a *New York Times Magazine* article published in October 1972, he noted that the melting pot in the U.S. failed when it came to the color of one's skin. In the country's history, Native Americans were slaughtered, Japanese were interred during World War II by an otherwise liberal president, people with brown skin were taken advantage of as farm labor, and Blacks still deal with inequalities more than a century after emancipation. The need for civil rights reform runs deep.

While Hesburgh personally opposed the Vietnam War, he took a stern stance against violent student demonstrations on campus in 1970, declaring that such protesters would be given six minutes to disperse before getting suspended or expelled.

Hesburgh spoke to more than two thousand demonstrators at Notre Dame on May 4, 1970, the same day four students were killed at Kent State University in Ohio. He read a handwritten statement that came to be known as the Hesburgh Declaration, which called for the "withdrawal of our military forces at the earliest moment" from Vietnam and for "renewing the quality of American life." Nonetheless, students went on a largely peaceful strike for seven days, ending in a demonstration before the Memorial Library, where they gazed toward the arms of Christ reaching out as they stood for peace, inside the library concourse and gathered twenty-three thousand signatures endorsing the Hesburgh Declaration. The rest of the war passed fairly peacefully at Notre Dame.

He reflected on student unrest in a commencement speech at USC in 1968. He tried to understand and explain campus revolt as grassroots movements where students, feeling helpless to end the war in Vietnam, in which high school classmates were dying, sought reform where they were—in the universities.

This was always Hesburgh's approach; he sought understanding even when he could not condone. Maybe especially then.

Once again, Father Hesburgh demonstrated his immense capacity to hear and understand the concerns of others. This is a major test of character that many of us repeatedly fail.

He often spoke about character and how to form it, from both a Christian and lay perspective.

He identified in a 1952 speech the three most important qualities of a leader of character: "professional competence, personal excellence, and social responsibility." Not only did Father Hesburgh embody all of these throughout his life and career, but he also ceaselessly preached their importance and value.

Let's examine each one briefly. As we've seen throughout this book, the most successful leaders have reached recognition in an organization or company or scientific profession through hard work and sometimes a little luck. Some people are geniuses, most aren't. They have gained the respect of their colleagues and often the public at large because of their achievements.

But they also are respected because of the way they handle themselves personally, apart from their profession. These two aspects sometimes merge, as we've seen through the towering and evident humanity of Nelson Mandela and Mother Teresa, for example, or in the humility and personality Jimmy Stewart brought to all his film roles.

The final mark of a leader is a commitment to social responsibility, through the activism of the Suffragettes or the sacrifices of the nurses we've seen earlier, for instance. Leadership means little unless it goes somewhere, most often to help others. Hesburgh often said students should be activists off campus as well as on, and he lived by that creed himself.

Father Hesburgh was particularly proud of his decision to accept women students in 1972, after attempts to merge with the neighboring women's school, Saint Mary's College, failed. This was three years after Yale did the same, and it's an understatement to say it wasn't universally popular with the then all-male alumni. But Hesburgh was firm that the student body would be better, maybe to the surprise of many, with this fundamental change.

He was also interested in science and especially flight and the space program. He served on the U.S. National Science Board, appointed by President Eisenhower, and as a Vatican representative to the International Atomic Energy Agency. He occasionally flew in advanced Air Force jets, going as far as the edge of space.

Hesburgh believed that the Creator had endowed man with curiosity and freedom to explore His creations. "The most insistent and important question of every human child is 'Why?,'" he said.

In a 1990 speech, he reflected on the iconic photo of Earth taken from space by the Apollo astronauts. The photo illustrated, he said, that the Earth belonged to everyone and we should live in harmony; that the Earth is unique in space, and that we all must work to preserve the habitat God has given us.

He saw no conflict between his scientific interest and his religious beliefs.

Hesburgh's autobiography, *God, Country, Notre Dame* (University of Notre Dame Press, 1990), was a best seller. It's worth reading and gives great insight into his character.

On leadership, Hesburgh espoused fundamentals. He thought one shouldn't make decisions because they were cheap or easy but rather because they were right. He believed in the show, not tell, approach: It's easier to exemplify values than teach them.

He believed in the power of proper leadership to change minds. Almost all of his talks and speeches to students emphasized the leadership points of strength, intelligence, and courage as he urged young people to become that sort of leader in academia, business, or life.

Leadership means getting things done, by looking at many possible solutions and picking the best one based on your personal ethics and character. No choice can be made in a spiritual or ethical vacuum. Leadership means convincing others to share your vision and then together accomplish it.

Obviously his faith colored his attitude toward leadership. He knew that the world was full of both saints and sinners, and that most great leaders at some time touched the latter category. He wore his faith lightly, not afraid to laugh when appropriate. He realized that not everyone shared either his faith or his devotion to it, and he was comfortable with that.

Ted Hesburgh died in 2015 at the age of ninety-seven. The headline of his *New York Times* obituary said he "Lifted Notre Dame and Advised Presidents." Both statements are true and insufficient.

He advised and lifted all of us.

Lessons

Theodore Hesburgh's career offers lessons in how transparency can transform a university and the world.

- Leading is a lot different from just believing. A leader's faith inspires others.

- Liberal or conservative can be misleading labels. Judge people on how their actions correspond with your worldview.
- Make the most of any opportunity that comes your way. Producing results from day one can help you, for example, remain president of a great university for thirty-five years.
- Religious faith is no barrier to success; espousing faith is one sign of transparency and integrity.
- Try to understand the reasons behind other's points of views and actions, especially if they differ from your own.

Chapter Ten

TRANSCENDENCE

All the information we need to address a problem is inside ourselves already, provided—of course!—we are first able to reach a level of unity with our deepest selves.

—S. P. Hinduja

S. P. Hinduja

I'll never forget the day S. P. Hinduja walked into my midtown Manhattan office and sat down in front of my desk.

"My name is S. P. Hinduja and I've come with my grandson Karam," he announced. "What office should he sit in?"

I was stunned. It was the first time we had met, though I knew of his reputation. Everyone did; he was the wealthiest man in Great Britain. His grandson, right before me, was all of fifteen years old.

"Three offices down," I managed to say.

"That will be fine," S. P. replied. He had told Karam that my mentorship would be valuable for him professionally. S. P. stood to escort Karam down the hall.

The visit and request—well, not really a request, more like a gesture of respect and foresight—took me by surprise, but my international public relations firm was busy, and we soon found plenty of projects of increasing complexity for Karam to complete. He possessed an innate intelligence and before long was one of our top interns.

Now, many years later, Karam Hinduja leads the international bank in Switzerland founded by his grandfather. His mother,

Shanu Hinduja, is chairman of the board, the first woman to hold such a position. When Karam became the CEO of the Geneva-headquartered bank in 2020, he changed the name from Hinduja Bank to S. P. Hinduja Banque Privée, in honor of the family patriarch.

S. P. would never command such an honor from a family member or anyone; the naming was born out of immense respect for a unique person.

Unique is a word that should not be overused, as it would lose its meaning. If everything is unique, then nothing is. The word, however, aptly applies to S. P. Though not tall in stature, his presence was towering.

His uniqueness did not come from his formidable wealth, reportedly in the billions. It arose from his character, which embodied many of the traits we have discussed in this book. Leadership, innovation, loyalty, and integrity—plus modesty, self-discipline, inquisitiveness, and a profound caring and respect for humanity combined in such a way to create the quality of transcendence.

How did S. P. do this? Let's look at his life.

Srichand Parmanand Hinduja was born in 1935 in the area of India that would become Pakistan after it was partitioned twelve years later. He was the second of five sons of Parmanand Deepchand and Jamuna Hinduja; they had twelve children, nine of whom survived to adulthood.

Parmanand had established a trading business with his two brothers in India, which set the foundation for the family enterprises. Financial market turmoil after World War I compelled Parmanand to look for new opportunities and form trade partnerships in Iran for goods such as tea, spices, and textiles.

Srichand, whom everyone called S. P., listened; he said he was always more interested in the conversation of grown-ups than those of his own age group, his daughter Vinoo recollected.

By the 1950s, Parmanand and his two oldest sons, Girdhar

and S. P., were operating textile mills to process cotton and silk, and plants to manufacture items such as plywood.

Parmanand set a philanthropic example that S. P. would emulate: Parmanand established a trust for the family's education, which founded a school and a college; he established a refugee center during the partition and because gradually the refugees often arrived injured, it slowly converted into a twenty-bed clinic. Many years later, SP converted it into a 350-bed tertiary hospital, which got named National Hospital and today is known as P. D. Hinduja Hospital & Medical Research Centre—a dream of S.P. to institutionalize health care in India.

By any measure, the family was successful. But Girdhar and S. P. began to take the enterprises to another level in 1957, when they started buying the international rights to Bollywood movies and promoting them around the world.

Sadly, Girdhar died of leukemia in 1962 at the young age of thirty-two. Parmanand died in 1971 and Jamuna in 1973, thus S. P. became the leader and patriarch (Karta) of the family.

He was constantly expanding the enterprises, not necessarily for the wealth but for the challenge. In 1978, S. P. established Amas SA Finance in Switzerland, which became Amas Bank, then Hinduja Bank, and as we have seen finally the S. P. Hinduja Banque Privée with his grandson Karam at the helm.

"When I was a child, seven or eight years old, I dreamed I would someday own a bank in Switzerland, that bank would overlook a lake and I, in turn, would also own a chalet on a nearby mountain," S. P. once wrote in his private reflections. "A dream not likely to happen! No Indian-owned bank had ever opened for business in Switzerland and there was no reason to think one ever would." But decades later he made it happen, and today the bank has a network all over Switzerland and a presence in Dubai, Mumbai, New York, and elsewhere. S. P. focused on possibilities, not limitations.

By the 1970s, the Hindujas controlled a large portion of the nearly $4 billion annual trade between India and Iran, but the

Iranian Revolution in 1979 prompted them to move many of their business interests out of the country. S. P. relocated to London.

With S. P.'s leadership, the Hinduja Group acquired Gulf Oil (outside of the U.S., Spain, and Portugal) in 1984 and Ashok Leyland, India's second-largest truck manufacturer, through a partnership with Iveco in 1987. Eventually S. P. would expand into IT, software, media, communications, and other industries.

He built businesses but operated them as a custodian, not as an owner. If you fail to detach yourself from personal gains, then your ego will get in the way and you will lose focus, he believed.

Always function with honesty, he told his children. Invest in your employees and take care of their economic growth, and they, too, will invest in the organization.

S. P. developed five principles that guided his business enterprises as well as his personal life: work to give; word is bond; advance fearlessly; act local, think global; and partnership for growth.

I won't go into all the business dealings here—it would take a book—but suffice to say S. P. made his family exceedingly wealthy. Yet that did not change his core character.

Most important to him was family. He felt a responsibility not only to care for them but also to teach them. Knowledge is power. With his wife, Madhu, he would have three children: daughters Shanu and Vinoo and a son, Dharam.

Karam, Shanu's son, recalled his grandfather's office and the ornate desk, similar to a Louis XIV style, where he conducted business. Personal life and work were inseparable for S. P. He had a smaller, exact replica made of his desk for Karam and placed it near his in the office. While Karam did his homework at the desk, he was receiving a master class in how to conduct business. He also learned this valuable lesson: observe.

Lavanya, Shanu's daughter, spent much time with her grandparents after moving to London at the age of fourteen. She, too, learned about business from her grandfather, who showed her that her mind and will were her only limitations. If she believed in her inner strength and power, he told her, then anything was possible. To help her see this, he would always recount stories of powerful women, such as his own mother or historical figures such as Jhansi ki Rani. He loved telling the story of this queen whose kingdom was under siege but managed to fight and rode out with her baby on her back to escape imminent death.

To S. P. there were no differences according to gender, a belief that was empowering to his daughters and granddaughter. Keep in mind, this is how it should be, though history shows us that such equality is not a given.

"Why the self, family, and work life are kept apart has never made sense to me," S. P. reflected. "To me, they are the same, and of the three by far the most important is family."

Philanthropy has long been a hallmark of the family. Shanu Hinduja was a board member of the Hinduja Foundation, which was founded in 1968 by her grandfather as the umbrella organization to support and fund the family's philanthropy.

For just a few examples of the foundation's good work around the world: it established the Hinduja Laboratory within the Endocrine Unit at Massachusetts General Hospital in Boston (1984); in cooperation with the Asia Society, founded the Center for India-US Education in New York (1991) to strengthen India-American understanding through educational activities; in the U.K. the Hinduja Cambridge Trust was formed to provide scholarships to worthy Indian students studying for postgraduate degrees at the University of Cambridge (1991); in memory of Dharam, who passed away in 1992, established the Dharam Hinduja Institute of Indic Research in India and at the University of Cambridge and Columbia University, devoted to finding modern-day applications for the Vedic scriptures and traditions, including yoga and ayurveda (1994); created the Millennium Pledge for Better Multicultural Understanding, launched at Alexandra Palace by then Prime Minister Tony Blair (1999); became a founding member of the Prince Albert II of Monaco

Foundation, dedicated to the prevention of the harmful effects of climate change (2006).

To this day, care for the environment is one of Shanu's passions.

S. P. did more than contribute financially to help others; he lived his life in a way that gave dignity and notice to all.

Shanu recalled that when the family lived in Mumbai, India, her father would often join pickup games of cricket with players from the nearby slum. Social standing didn't matter to him—he saw people, not class.

This quality defused difficult situations in what, to some, seemed like magic.

One time on a long international flight, the attendant was surprisingly brusque with everyone. Lavanya recalled that her grandfather wanted to understand why she was having a bad day; he genuinely wanted to form a connection and try to be helpful. S. P. started a conversation by asking questions: What did the flight attendant like about her job? What made her pursue this career? What's the most difficult part of it? Where was she from? With his sincere, nonconfrontational gaze, he continued to speak *with* her, not *at* her. Before long, the attendant was visibly in a better spot. He was an alchemist, Lavanya said.

In all your interactions, try to see others as individuals with their own hopes, worries, and experiences. Try to relate as a fellow human being.

His appreciation of the fine arts and respect for the world's religions melded in a remarkable way.

He was the first Indian to be granted a banking license in Switzerland; he wanted that bank not only to stand *out* but also to stand *for* something greater. For the 1994 inauguration of the Amas Bank in Geneva (which his grandson would later lead and name for him), S. P. commissioned the renowned Indian painter M. F. Husain to create the *Theorama* series of panels representing the nine main religions of the world—Vedic, Islam, Christianity, Judaism, Buddhism, Jainism, Sikhism, Zoroastrianism, and Taoism—with a tenth depicting Humanism. Can you imagine the impact of such a gesture of religious tolerance? It was at once grand and humbling. The paintings remain on the walls of the bank in Geneva.

S. P. was a man of self-discipline. Every day, since he was a teenager, he would rise between four and five a.m.

"Why do routine, and discipline matter?" he wrote. "The answer is that with both serving as your foundation, you can actually get things done!"

When he was a teenager he would rise early, go to work at the market selling textiles, then to school, then to his father's office and help him. "He believed you don't build something if you don't work for it," Vinoo told me.

As an adult, his daily routine included time for meditation and brisk walks outdoors. The internal and the physical. Connecting with nature was a source of strength.

His morning walks were legendary. Both Karam and Lavanya, though two generations younger, recalled they could hardly keep up with him. Smart people who would want to do business with him knew that if they got up early they could find him walking around St. James's Park in London and thus gain an audience—if they could keep up.

S. P.'s walks were more than physical exercise, although he was keen to stay fit. He loved sports, tennis in particular. As he fed his mind, he also took care of his body. The right food was important to S. P.; he was a vegetarian and consumed only the freshest ingredients. Wherever he went, he always brought his chef or his freshly prepared vegetarian meal, which he would share with everyone, who often were more excited about his food than what they were being served. He even brought his own meals when Queen Elizabeth II would invite him to dinner at Buckingham Palace. (They were neighbors.)

S. P. was always true to himself, he did not adjust his values or priorities depending upon whom he was with. Not even the queen of England! Remember that, in the likely event you should feel pressured to conform your values to those around you.

The daily walks, wherever he was, were his grounding, his connection to nature. He would bring some bread for the birds, some peanuts for the squirrels, as he did when he walked his son to school. The animals came to expect these gifts. Shanu recalled that one time her father was ill and could not take his morning walks. Apparently, he was missed. Within a few days, a certain squirrel instead came to him—it would sit on the windowsill, looking in—every day until S. P. could resume his walks.

"If I have any mission, it is to help others blend their lives with nature," wrote one of the world's wealthiest men, "in the same way nature has been my guide since I was a child."

As you build and nurture your character, do not separate yourself from nature. We get tethered to our computers, tied to our smartphones, and hours can go by in the name of work without getting up or even looking out a window. That's not good! Make time in your schedule for a walk outside, to listen to the birds, to feel the sun's warmth. And be present in the moment to appreciate the connection to the natural world.

Not everyone will reach the quality of transcendence to go beyond normal limits. But it is worth trying. And you can begin by perfecting the many aspects of character we have discussed in this book.

S. P. Hinduja passed away in 2023 at the age of eighty-seven, only a few months after his partner in life, Madhu. His legacy lives on through his businesses and many charitable causes, but most of all in his children and grandchildren. They knew him intimately because he always took the time to share himself with family.

His grandchildren Karam and Lavanya spoke at his memorial service of the "essence" of S. P.'s way of life:

"To remind ourselves, as he always did, to connect with our hearts, to connect with each other from a place of truth, and to connect to our shared planet. To show up as our true selves and realize the potential for change we can bring about in every task we undertake, big or small."

Lessons

- Always seek the humanity in another person. Treat them with respect, no matter their circumstances in life.
- Be self-disciplined; this will enable you to achieve your goals.
- No matter the situation, be true to yourself and your values.
- See the possibilities, not the limitations.
- Make your impact in ways of lasting value and meaning—the original paintings for the bank come to mind—instead of a big splash that is soon forgotten.
- Connect with nature; do not let yourself get separated from the world of which we are all a part.
- Care for your family in ways that are empowering and ennobling. Define family as you wish; it doesn't always have to be by genetics.

Chapter Eleven

LESSONS

Perfection of character is this: to live each day as if it were your last, without frenzy, without apathy, without pretense.
—Marcus Aurelius, *Meditations*

To end the book, let's recall the various lessons I've picked out from the character of the people I've profiled.

General Powell's thirteen rules speak for themselves, but here's my take on some of them:

- Character manifests itself through both word and deed.
- It's best to lead by example, and that example should be consistent.
- Leaders should be consistent but not stubborn.
- It's not only allowed but vital to change your mind and your actions when the facts change.
- Your colleagues, staff, or friends know when you're being totally honest or bluffing. Don't bluff.
- Be optimistic but realistic. Find the aspects of a situation or problem that are promising and pursue those.
- A leader considers criticism but isn't cowed or overwhelmed by it.
- Self-doubt can be healthy when recognized and controlled.
- People yearn to be led, but not bullied.

- Kindness, such as speaking someone's native language if you can, is the best icebreaker.
- Be visible. Don't sulk in your tent.
- Yelling rarely helps. Be firm but polite when dealing with employees or clients or friends.

Here are some character lessons you can draw from the life and work of Valéry Giscard d'Estaing:

Defeat strengthens character and can breed later triumph. Giscard did valuable work on European unity after his defeat in the 1981 French presidential election, remaining active in the French and European parliaments, promoting the euro, and helping draft a European constitution.

Honesty and openness in relationships are vital character traits and can produce unexpected results. Today's Europe would not be the same had Giscard not developed his very special relationship with Helmut Schmidt.

Experience leads to insight. By keeping active in European affairs and frequently meeting other leaders, Giscard understood in the late 1980s that the Soviet Union couldn't survive as then constituted. By the time it dissolved in 1991, he was virtually alone in predicting, correctly, that Poland and Hungary would join NATO by the end of the century.

Formality can serve a purpose. While sometimes dismissed as haughty by Frenchmen and foreigners alike, Giscard remained widely respected until his death, at age ninety-four, in 2020. Nobody really expected him to take off his tie in public.

Anwar Sadat's unique life offers several lessons on courage.

- If you're doing the right thing, do it despite the consequences.
- Think big. Many things haven't been done because nobody's tried them before.
- Think beyond local boundaries. Many decisions and actions have implications well beyond the local.

- Be patient. The Camp David Accords took thirteen days of painstaking negotiations.
- Communicate. Leadership doesn't exist in a vacuum.
- Stick to your guns even when facing hostile audiences. Honesty and persuasion will win them over.

While none of us is likely to be canonized a saint, we can learn a lot from Mother Teresa's life and works.

- Don't allow any space between what you do and what you say. People will follow your actions and will know immediately if your words don't match them.
- Use your faith. It is not just thoughts or words.
- Leaders come in all shapes and sizes. And they aren't all generals or presidents.

Dwight Eisenhower led as a soldier and politician through the quality and transparency of his actions.

- Great leaders aren't necessarily flashy, but an air of quiet authority makes them effective.
- Slow and steady wins the race.
- The character of leaders and commanders is what inspires respect.
- Shouting won't compensate for poor character.
- Hard truths need to be stated firmly and calmly, backed by facts.

Steve Jobs didn't just change our world through the products he unleashed at Apple, his too-short life offers a number of lessons.

- Connect the dots. Reflect on what has happened in your life to get you where you are, and how you can use that knowledge to plan your future.
- Learn to say no when saying yes would lead you down a

false path or distract you from what you are concentrating on. Do it gracefully.

- Don't settle. Stay hungry. Stay foolish. These are simple ideas but very hard to integrate into our lives. School, work, parents, and friends all seem to have rules that stifle creativity. The line between bending and breaking these rules—asserting your individuality without hurting others or yourself—can be a fine one.
- Don't lose faith. If you've done the research, experiments, field testing, polling, fact checking, or whatever convinces you that your ideas are worth pursuing, take any setbacks as motivation to get up and try again. The world may have written Jobs off when he was fired from Apple, but he never wrote himself off.

Frederick Banting made one of the great discoveries in medicine, and how he did it and what happened next offers great lessons.

- Inspiration can come at any time, even after a bad night's sleep. When it does, jump on it.
- Many experiments or marketing ideas or new product trials fail. Success usually comes only from repeated failure.
- Unselfishness is a powerful character trait. Banting wanted to share insulin with those who needed it.
- Always spread around credit. When the Nobel Prize committee didn't recognize his colleague Charles Best, Banting did, sharing the prize with him.

Walt Disney created some of the best-loved characters in entertainment and then grew his company into a global empire. His life has many lessons.

- Innovation requires both inspiration and insight, as Disney displayed when inventing all those characters and knowing that he was marketing to the adults with money who wanted wholesome entertainment for their children and themselves.

- Set your imagination free. Steamboat Willie to Sleeping Beauty's Castle to Luke Skywalker.
- Learn from your mistakes. When kicked in the teeth, get back up and keep fighting.
- Never hector, lecture, or talk down to kids. Let them love to learn and to grow.
- Be aware of what's influenced your decisions and stay humble and grounded. "It all started with a mouse."

Nelson Mandela's life after being released from twenty-seven years in prison is a lesson for us all.

- Don't get mad, get even. Good winners make victory all the more sweet.
- Never give up when your cause is just.
- Know that you have support, from friends, family, and coworkers, even when times seem dire.
- Strength is character.

Václav Havel, like Nelson Mandela, went from prison to the presidency of his country, although on a different path. The lessons:

- Don't take yourself seriously all the time. Self-deprecation can be a tool to express a resilient character.
- Be prepared for the unexpected. You're unlikely to be suddenly named president, but if that unexpected promotion or acceptance to your number one university choice comes through, be ready to accept and perform.
- Think beyond the immediate. There are generally bigger-picture implications of your actions.

Susan B. Anthony's and Emmeline Pankhurst's passionate advocacy of women's right to vote has lessons for us all.

- It can take a long time to change a society. Courage, patience, and resilience not only impress others but also eventually lead to change.
- Suffragettes in both the U.S. and the U.K. resisted the police and caused property damage to attract attention. Do you agree with these tactics if the cause is just?
- Leaders act, they don't just speak.
- Sometimes a leader will cement the support of one group—say, women—before trying to add the support of another group—say, men. If done properly, such a tactic is additive, not divisive.

Stephen Hawking's extraordinary example of the mind overcoming near paralysis of the body to make world-changing discoveries holds valuable lessons.

- The brain is the source of character. Disabilities can be overcome with a strong-enough will.
- Communication is essential to innovation. Discoveries need to be widely known and understood. The form of communication matters little—it can be a tinny mechanized voice—so long as the content is compelling.
- Curiosity is everything. Even if you don't throw a party and invite everyone after it's over to see if time travel exists, try lots of things that you wonder about.
- There is no such thing as a stupid question.
- If you ever think life has dealt you a bad hand, think of Stephen Hawking in his wheelchair, twitching a facial muscle to communicate. Do you have the resilience to face your problems?

Margaret Chase Smith's life offers lessons of courage and integrity as well as breaking barriers.

- Speaking your mind might not always be popular but it will win you respect.
- A broken barrier is no guarantee of success or necessarily an indication of strong character.
- Actions must follow.
- Bullies rarely stand up to being called out.
- Whether Mark Twain actually said it or not, history really does rhyme. Seeing parallels to past events is a useful tool for understanding.

Bill Russell taught lessons every day on and off the court.

- Grace, integrity, and hard work can overcome any barrier.
- While athletics have long offered the opportunity for the underprivileged to advance in society, the relatively few who have done so have had the strength, determination, and confidence to overcome barriers—vital character traits.
- Life is more than any profession, including professional sports. To be the best among thousands of talented engineers, athletes, or scholars requires a force of will we often see as character.

Julia Child offered not only cooking lessons but also life lessons.

- Nobody can prevent you from breaking a barrier except yourself. Whether it's running a marathon or cooking a four-course gourmet meal, it won't happen unless you train for it and then try it.
- Jump in. Child knew no one and spoke little French when she arrived in Paris with her husband. When she left, she was a Francophone who could cook, and had friends who helped her write her books and create her TV shows.
- Fail. Burn a few vol-au-vents before figuring it out.

Winston Churchill's lessons are indelible. Courage. Inspiration. Doggedness.

- Leaders inspire by displaying courage, both in word and deed.
- Courage gives leaders the resiliency to bounce back after defeat.
- People know when leaders are being honest with them, especially when they can see the truth themselves.

Arthur Ashe displayed lessons of courage with every backhand and every action of his various foundations.

- You don't need to shout to make your voice heard.
- Courage comes from strong grounding in what is right and wrong.
- Rather than complain, fight against adversity.
- Arguing may get you attention but moving on without arguing gets you a stadium named after yourself.

Lou Gehrig taught lessons with his baseball bat on the field and his courage in the face of his devastating illness.

- Life isn't fair. It takes courage to count your blessings despite bad breaks.
- Humility in the face of success will inspire others to admire and follow you.
- Courage is sometimes knowing when to stop.

Florence Nightingale and Edith Cavell revolutionized nursing, under fire, and in Cavell's case at the expense of her life. Both offer lessons.

- Courage can come from anywhere.
- Heroism often arises from simple humanity.
- Professionalism—in nursing, for example—saves lives.

Eleanor Roosevelt started from a high perch as First Lady and became one of the most famous women in U.S. history. Her lessons:

- Pick a cause and stick with it.
- If you have a platform, exploit its influence for all it's worth.
- Leadership emerges when times are hardest.
- Starting in a privileged position is great, but it's what you do from there that counts.

John Wooden's loyalty to his players as human beings as well as athletes, and his loyalty to basketball, offer valuable lessons.

- Loyalty comes from trust. Trust comes from honesty.
- Try to inspire the loyalty that John Wooden did in Kareem Abdul-Jabbar: loyalty and friendship that endured for fifty years.
- Teamwork is a pure example of loyalty to one's team-mates and oneself.
- The best way to keep winning is to never have to talk about it.
- Talent is wasted without leadership.

John McCain embodied loyalty to his fellow prisoners and his country, providing lessons we all need.

- Be magnanimous in victory and gracious in defeat.
- Loyalty to yourself and colleagues is the foremost test of character.
- Your loyalty will often overshadow the exact details of your actions or votes or statements at any time.

Daniel Patrick Moynihan's distinguished career as a diplomat and U.S. senator was based squarely on his ability to project integrity with every word he said. That's a lesson for us all.

- The best way to display integrity is to tell the truth fully, plainly, and, if possible, eloquently.
- Scorn for an opponent's argument should be used sparingly. Facts are better.
- As the man said, you're entitled to your own opinion, but not your own facts.

Margaret Thatcher, through integrity and passion, changed Britain in many ways, offering many lessons.

- Don't be "for turning." When you feel you are right, defend your ideas.
- Don't allow self-confidence to turn into arrogance. State your case firmly and clearly, without snide remarks or condescension.
- Never give up on core fundamentals. It took Mrs. Thatcher a decade to see some of her ideas, like the poll tax, implemented.

Paul Volcker commanded every room he entered. His life offers lessons on how to do the same.

- Always explain, never complain.
- Authority comes from backing up your words with actions that work.
- Be aware of opposing opinions—such as a two-by-four delivered to your office—but stick to your guns if you're convinced you are right.
- Politics—be they internal company or national politics—can make life miserable. Carry on through them.

Katharine Graham's life was one of constantly learning lessons and applying them to aid transparency and the free press.

- Transparency is a virtue unto itself, leading to honesty and integrity.

- Truth-telling can be hard and sometimes costly, but it's always worth it.
- The backing of the top boss, even if it's in the shadows, is the most powerful motivational tool in any organization.

What you saw on-screen with Jimmy Stewart was what you got. There are lessons in that.

- Transparency is closely related to honesty and integrity. WYSIWYG.
- Friends say Jimmy Stewart was the same on-screen and off, walking the dogs, eating lunch on Wall Street, flying model airplanes with Henry Fonda, or accepting a medal from fellow actor Ronald Reagan. That's transparency—and character.
- Bring the same temperament to everything you do, be it acting or flying a jet bomber.

Theodore Hesburgh's career offers lessons in how transparency can transform a university and the world.

- Leading is a lot different from just believing. A leader's faith inspires others.
- Liberal or conservative can be misleading labels. Judge people on how their actions correspond with your worldview.
- Make the most of any opportunity that comes your way. Producing results from day one can help you, for example, remain president of a great university for thirty-five years.
- Religious faith is no barrier to success; espousing faith is one sign of transparency and integrity.

S. P. Hinduja incorporated many of the values and traits that we have discussed to achieve transcendence. It was vitally important that he remained true to himself, no matter the situation.

- Be self-disciplined. This will enable you to achieve your goals.
- See the possibilities, not the limitations.
- Connect with nature; do not let yourself get separated from the world of which we are all a part.

EPILOGUE

A quote from John McCain, once addressing a student group, seems a fitting way to end this book. He said:

"You have at hand many examples of good character from whom you will have learned the lessons by which you can live your own lives. You are blessed. Make the most of it."

If you do take the advice of Senator McCain and me and try to emulate some of the people you've just read about, here's another piece of advice: Don't try to emulate them all.

Nobody can do that.

It's better to pick one or two of these heroes and heroines in your particular area of interest or expertise and try to be like them. Also, I hope you'll go back and jot down a few stories or quotations that especially moved you and pass them along to family and friends and bear them in mind as you get on with your careers and lives.

There is a rich mix from which to choose, from Colin Powell to Father Theodore Hesburgh, by way of Mother Teresa, Nelson Mandela, Margaret Thatcher, Steve Jobs, S. P. Hinduja, and the others. I hope in each case you will use these profiles as starting points to learn more about these outstanding individuals.

If you do, I'm hopeful you will see ways to shape your character and those of the people around you.

As I said at the beginning, we desperately need more men and women of character in everything: from the local school board to the White House, from preschool to postgraduate education, from the corner pharmacy to the teaching hospital, from summer stock to Hollywood, from the neighborhood bodega to the Fortune 500.

The world will be a better place if we can all improve our character. I'm counting on you to get started.

ACKNOWLEDGMENTS

This book was inspired by my late sister, Mary Lou Shay, and by my good friend Roger Ailes, who passed away in 2017.

Each was passionate about upholding the values that have made Americans the most enterprising, caring, and forward-looking people on Earth. Each, in his or her own way, believed that now more than ever our nation and the world need to be reminded of what those values are.

Hence this book, which brings together a global group of men and women who, through the examples of their lives, illustrate what character is and how it can change the course of history for the better.

So many helped with the book.

This book would not be possible without the thoughtful research of Jacqueline Smith, Philip Revzin, and Robert Laird, whom I have worked with for many years. Each of them brings a unique quotient to all that they do, and it's my privilege to work with them. My colleague Jonathan Dedmon also provided an objective view. Working with him for nearly forty years has been a terrific experience.

Of course, Joan Avagliano, with whom I have worked with for decades, kept us all on track. Anthony Quiles-Roche and Yolanda Guzman supported the effort. Nataliya Lustig, Francine Benedetti, and Mirella DeMoura are three of the best in keeping me on deadline.

Michaela Hamilton, executive editor at Kensington, provided insight and direction that are parallel to none. I've never met a better editor. She continues to raise the bar for all to follow in the publishing world. Steve Zacharius, chairman, president, and CEO of Kensington, deserves special thanks for all he does for so many.

My wife, Jan, a painter of some caliber, deserves high praise for encouraging me to complete my nineteenth book and offering advice on all who are included in this volume.

No statement of acknowledgment would be complete without mention of my supportive family: My sister, Martha (and Cort); my sons, Geoffrey and Peter (and their wives Sabina and Julia); and my niece, Ricia Harding (and Paul and their sons, Chase and Christian). I hope our grandchildren, Bruce, Logan, and Hailey, will study those in this book and shape their futures accordingly.

NOTES AND SOURCES

Colin Powell

Thirteen Rules of Leadership: https://www.state.gov/dip-note-u-s-department-of-state-official-blog/colin-l-powells-thirteen-rules-of-leadership/

My American Journey, by Colin Powell with Joseph Persico (Random House, 1995)

It Worked For Me: In Life and Leadership, by Colin Powell with Tony Koltz (Harper, 2012)

Valéry Giscard d'Estaing

Le Pouvoir et la Vie, by Valéry Giscard d'Estaing (France Loisirs, 1988)

Anwar Sadat

Nobel Prize lecture: https://www.nobelprize.org/prizes/peace/1978/al-sadat/lecture/

Mother Teresa

Nobel Prize lecture: https://www.nobelprize.org/prizes/peace/1979/teresa/acceptance-speech/

Dwight D. Eisenhower

Farewell address: https://www.archives.gov/milestone-documents/president-dwight-d-eisenhowers-farewell-address

"Cross of Iron" speech: https://www.eisenhowerlibrary.gov/sites/default/files/file/chance_for_peace.pdf

Crusade in Europe: A Personal Account of World War II, by Dwight D. Eisenhower (Doubleday, 1948)

Eisenhower: Soldier and President, by Stephen E. Ambrose (Simon & Schuster, 1991)

Steve Jobs

Steve Jobs, by Walter Isaacson (Simon & Schuster, 2011)

Commencement address, Stanford University, June 12, 2005, https://news.stanford.edu/stories/2005/06/youve-got-find-love-jobs-says

Frederick Banting

Breakthrough: Elizabeth Hughes, the Discovery of Insulin, and the Making of a Medical Miracle, by Thea Cooper and Arthur Ainsberg (St. Martin's Press, 2010)

Nobel Prize lecture: https://www.nobelprize.org/prizes/medicine/1923/banting/lecture/

Walt Disney

Walt Disney: The Triumph of the American Imagination, by Neal Gabler (Vintage, 2007)

Disney's Land: Walt Disney and the Invention of the Amusement Park That Changed the World, by Richard Snow (Scribner, 2019)

Nelson Mandela

Nobel Prize lecture: https://www.nobelprize.org/prizes/peace/1993/mandela/lecture/

Long Walk to Freedom: The Autobiography of Nelson Mandela, by Nelson Mandela (Little, Brown, 1994)

Václav Havel

The Power of the Powerless: Citizens Against the State in Central Eastern Europe, by Václav Havel (Routledge, 2009)

Speech to Congress: February 21, 1990,
https://www.havelcenter.org

Susan B. Anthony

https://susanb.org
Failure Is Impossible: Susan B. Anthony in Her Own Words, by Lynn Sherr (Crown, 1995)

Emmeline Pankhurst

"Freedom or Death" speech, November 13, 1913, https://awpc.cattcenter.iastate.edu/2017/03/09/freedom-or-death-part-1-nov-13-1913/

Stephen Hawking

A Brief History of Time, by Stephen Hawking (Bantam, 1998)
The Universe in a Nutshell, by Stephen Hawking (Bantam, 2001)
The Grand Design, by Stephen Hawking and Leonard Mlodinow (Bantam, 2010)

Margaret Chase Smith

"Declaration of Conscience" speech, June 1, 1950, https://www.senate.gov/artandhistory/history/resources/pdf/Smith Declaration.pdf
Politics of Conscience: A Biography of Margaret Chase Smith, by Patricia Ward Wallace (Praeger, 1995)

Bill Russell

Go Up for Glory, by Bill Russell, as told to William McSweeny (Coward-McCann, 1966)

Julia Child

Mastering the Art of French Cooking, by Julia Child with Louisette Bertholle and Simone Beck (Knopf, 1961, 1970)

Winston Churchill

The World Crisis, by Winston Churchill (Scribner, 1923)

The Second World War, by Winston Churchill (Houghton Mifflin, 1948–1953)

A History of the English Speaking Peoples, by Winston Churchill (Cassell, 1956–1958)

His Complete Speeches, 1897–1963, by Winston Churchill (Chelsea House, 1974)

Arthur Ashe

Advantage Ashe, by Arthur Ashe, as told to Clifford George Gewecke, Jr. (Coward-McCann, 1967)

Portrait in Motion: The Arthur Ashe Diary, by Arthur Ashe, with Frank Deford (Houghton Mifflin, 1975)

Off the Court, by Arthur Ashe, with Neil Amdur (New American Library, 1981)

A Hard Road to Glory: A History of the African-American Athlete vols. 1–3, by Arthur Ashe, with the assistance of Kip Branch, Oceania Chalk, and Francis Harris (Amistad, 1988–1993)

Days of Grace: A Memoir, by Arthur Ashe, with Arnold Rampersad (Alfred A. Knopf, 1993)

Arthur Ashe on Tennis: Strokes, Strategy, Traditions, Players, Psychology, and Wisdom, Arthur Ashe, with Alexander McNab (HarperCollins, 1996)

Lou Gehrig

"Luckiest Man" speech, July 4, 1939, https://baseballhall. org/discover-more/stories/baseball-history/lou-gehrig-luckiest -man

Luckiest Man: The Life and Death of Lou Gehrig, by Jonathan Eig (Simon & Schuster, 2005)

Florence Nightingale

Florence Nightingale: The Courageous Life of the Legendary Nurse, by Catherine Reef (Clarion, 2016)

"Santa Filomena," by Henry Wadsworth Longfellow,
https://www.simple-poetry.com/poems/santa-filomena
-75194533373

Edith Cavell
Fatal Decision: Edith Cavell, World War I Nurse, by Terri Arthur (HenschelHAUS, 2014)

Eleanor Roosevelt
https://fdrlibrary
The Autobiography of Eleanor Roosevelt, by Eleanor Roosevelt (Harper Perennial, 2014)

John Wooden
TheWoodenEffect.com (WoodenEffect website, maintained by Craig Impelman and *Success* magazine)
Wooden on Leadership, by John Wooden, with Steve Jamison (McGraw Hill, 2005)
Coach Wooden's Pyramid of Success, by John Wooden, with Jay Carty (Baker Pub Group, 2005)

John McCain
Faith of My Fathers: A Family Memoir, with Mark Salter (Random House, 1999)
Character Is Destiny: Inspiring Stories Every Young Person Should Know and Every Adult Should Remember, with Mark Salter (Random House, 2005)
The Restless Wave, Good Times, Just Causes, Great Fights, and Other Appreciations, with Mark Salter (Simon & Schuster, 2018)

Daniel Patrick Moynihan
"Fighting the Zionism Is Racism Lie," speech to the UN, November 10, 1975, https://unwatch.org/moynihans-moment-the-historic-1975-u-n-speech-in-response-to-zionism-is-racism/

Miles to Go: A Personal History of Social Policy (Harvard University Press, 1997)

Margaret Thatcher
The Downing Street Years, by Margaret Thatcher (Harper-Collins, 1993)

Margaret Thatcher: The Authorized Biography (vol. 1, *From Grantham to the Falklands*), by Charles Moore, (Vintage, 2015)

Margaret Thatcher: The Authorized Biography (vol. 2, *At Her Zenith: In London, Washington, and Moscow*), by Charles Moore (Knopf, 2016)

Margaret Thatcher: The Authorized Biography (vol. 3, *Herself Alone*), by Charles Moore (Knopf, 2019)

Paul Volcker
Keeping At It: The Quest for Sound Money and Good Government, by Paul Volcker with Christine Harper (PublicAffairs, 2018)

Katharine Graham
Personal History, by Katharine Graham (Knopf, 2017)

Jimmy Stewart
Jimmy Stewart: A Biography, by Marc Eliot (Crown, 2006)
Jimmy Stewart and His Poems (Crown, 1989)

Theodore Hesburgh
All quotes downloaded from Theodore Hesburgh archives, University of Notre Dame, https://sites.nd.edu/ndarchives /hesburgh-portal/ (November 2023). Used by permission.